Freshwater Fishes of New York State

A York State Book

Freshwater Fishes of New York State

A Field Guide

Robert G. Werner

SYRACUSE UNIVERSITY PRESS • 1980

THIS BOOK was published with the assistance of a grant from the John Ben Snow Foundation.

This research was sponsored (in part) by New York Sea Grant Institute under a grant from the Office of Sea Grant, National Oceanic and Atmospheric Administration (NOAA), U.S. Department of Commerce. The U.S. government is authorized to produce and distribute reprints for governmental purposes, notwithstanding any copyright notation appearing hereon.

ROBERT G. WERNER is Professor of Forest Zoology at State University of New York College of Environmental Science and Forestry at Syracuse.

Library of Congress Cataloging in Publication Data

Werner, Robert G
    Freshwater fishes of New York State.

    (A York State book)
    Includes bibliographies and index.
    1. Fishes, Fresh-water—New York (State)—Identification. 2. Fishes—New York (State)—Identification. I. Title.
QL628.N7W47   597.092'9747   80-17942
ISBN 0-8156-2222-8

Manufactured in the United States of America

Preface

THIS BOOK is a guide to the fishes of New York's lakes and streams for the amateur naturalist and fisherman. Nature has provided New York with more than 3½ million acres of lakes and 70,000 miles of streams, abundant habitat for many species of fish. What kinds of fishes live in these waters? How can they be identified? Where do they live? What do they eat? When do they spawn? How large do they get? *Freshwater Fishes of New York State* will provide answers to these questions and many others as well.

Included here are keys to the identification of all the freshwater fishes of New York State, along with discussions of the life history and distribution of 68 of the most common species. For those who would like to pursue any subject further a selected list of scientific studies, usually conducted in New York waters, is included. These papers will introduce the reader to the wealth of research that has been done on New York's fishes and will add much more detail to the account given here.

It is hoped that this book will assist the fisherman, conservationist, naturalist, or student to become more familiar with the extremely interesting and diverse fish fauna of New York and, as a result, lead us all to be more considerate of the fishes as we continue to modify their environment.

A book of this nature has been needed for some time. The most recent comprehensive attempt was in 1903, when T. H. Bean published *A Catalogue of the Fishes of New York*. Since Bean's time the New York State Conservation Department has conducted extensive biological surveys of the state's major watersheds, including exhaustive fish surveys by Dr. John Greeley. Unfortunately, this excellent work, published in 14 volumes from 1927 to 1940, is now out of print. There is no single work currently available which will provide a description of the freshwater fishes of the state useful to the layman.

Since all of the species of fish found in New York range well beyond the political boundaries of the state and most can be found over all of the northeastern United States and southeastern Canada, this book should be useful to residents and fishermen in neighboring states and provinces as well.

Many people have assisted in the preparation of *Freshwater Fishes of New York State*. Donald Squires, Director of New York's Sea Grant Program, and his staff, particularly John Judd, have been helpful and encouraging. The figures were drawn by Henry Schmidt, and the map was prepared by Dennis Carmichael with funds provided by New York Sea Grant. Suggestions made by Paul Neth of the New York Department of Environmental Conservation, Lavett Smith of the American Museum of Natural History, Neil Ringler of the New York State College of Environmental Science and Forestry, and Terry Finger of Oregon State University have been incorporated into the text. The monumental job of typing several drafts of the manuscript fell to Dorothy Schafer and Ruth Piatoff. Finally, I owe a considerable debt of gratitude to my wife, Jo, who created a climate conducive to the preparation of this work.

Spring 1980   RGW

Contents

Table

Freshwater Fishes of New York State

Introduction

AT LEAST 163 species of fish are known to live or spawn in the fresh waters of New York State. Add to that 30 or more marine species which make occasional forays into freshwater reaches of the Hudson River or Long Island streams and the total number of species approaches 200; 25 families and 16 orders are represented in the freshwater grouping alone. This great diversity results mainly from the variety of freshwater habitats in the state. Fish habitats include large lakes (Ontario and Erie), large rivers (Hudson and St. Lawrence), deep clear lakes (Champlain, George, and the Finger Lakes), soft-water lakes (Adirondack lakes), shallow productive lakes (Oneida and Chautauqua), and a myriad number of small lakes and streams.

Major Drainages of New York

Because freshwater fishes are confined to the network of streams and lakes that flow from the mountains to the sea, their distribution is heavily dependent upon the geography of drainage systems. Freshwater fishes cannot travel from one drainage to another since they cannot cross land or traverse the salty waters of the ocean. Consequently, their geographic distribution is restricted unless some outside agent such as man helps them overcome this barrier. Because of the important role drainage systems play in fish distribution, ichthyologists tend to think in terms of drainage basins rather than political boundaries.

The fresh waters of New York flow to the ocean via 6 major routes. Water in the southwestern corner of the state flows via the Allegheny River to the Ohio River and then down the Mississippi River to the Gulf

1

of Mexico. The central and northern part of the state drains to the north and ultimately reaches the ocean via the St. Lawrence River. This is the largest drainage system in the state, and it is often subdivided into the following subdrainages: Genesee River, Oswego River, Oswegatchie River, Black River, Raquette River, Lake Champlain, and the small streams directly tributary to Lake Erie and Lake Ontario. Water in the eastern portion of the state flows to the ocean via the Hudson River and its major tributary, the Mohawk. The southern part of New York is drained by two systems, the Susquehanna and Delaware. In addition, Long Island has many small streams that flow directly to the ocean, none reaching the size of the previously named systems. Finally, several minor systems drain small areas of the state. The Ramapo and Hackensack Rivers drain a small section in the southeastern part of the state between the Delaware and Hudson drainages, and numerous small streams drain from Westchester County directly into Long Island Sound. Thus, New York has 6 major drainages: Allegheny, St. Lawrence, Hudson, Delaware, Susquehanna, and Long Island; plus the minor drainages of the Ramapo, Hackensack, and Westchester County streams (see Figure 1).

Figure 1. Major drainage systems in New York

Distribution of New York Fishes

The distribution of fishes among the 6 major drainage systems and the subdrainages of the Great Lakes–St. Lawrence and Hudson systems is summarized in Table 1. This distribution is based on the biological surveys and certain known introductions such as the chinook and coho salmon into the Great Lakes and the elimination of some dubious records such as the spoonbill.

Naming Fishes

For many years scientists named plants and animals without any organized plan. In 1735, Carl Linnaeus changed all that. He suggested that we give each creature 2 names — the first its generic name to indicate its relationship to other closely related species, and the second the specific name which would distinguish it from all other species of that genus. He also proposed that Latin be used for these names since it was widely used by scholars at the time. Linnaeus' system has been used ever since by scientists throughout the world.

For example, the scientific name of the brook trout is *Salvelinus fontinalis*. *Salvelinus* is the name of the genus which includes the lake trout and arctic char, two species closely related to the brook trout. The species name is *fontinalis*, which distinguishes the brook trout from the lake trout and arctic char. The brook trout is the only animal in the world with this scientific name. In addition, *Salvelinus fontinalis* is the only zoologically correct name for this species. Any zoologist in the world, by consulting the appropriate references, could find a complete description of *Salvelinus fontinalis* and from that would know exactly what fish it was. The zoologist, however, might have some difficulty if he relied on common names, since this fish is also called speckled trout, native trout, squaretailed trout, eastern brook trout, and speckled char.

In the United States and Canada the American Fisheries Society has listed an accepted common name for each of the fishes along with its scientific name. This makes it possible for us to use common names without confusion. In this book, both the common and scientific names will be used initially, but in subsequent references only the common name recommended in "A List of Common and Scientific Names of Fishes from the United States and Canada," American Fisheries Society, Special Publication No. 6, will be used.

In addition to the scientific nomenclature developed by Linnaeus, biologists classify organisms according to their relationships with other

Distribution of New York Fishes

Key: ✓ = species present (indicated by a stylized fish symbol in the source table).

SPECIES	Allegheny	DRAINAGES — Great Lakes–St. Lawrence: Erie	Ontario	Oswego	Genesee	St. Lawrence	Oswegatchie and Black	Raquette	Champlain	Hudson	Delaware	Susquehanna	Long Island
Northern brook lamprey (*Ichthyomyzon fossor*)		✓											
Allegheny brook lamprey (*I. greeleyi*)	✓												
Silver lamprey (*I. unicuspis*)	✓	✓	✓	✓									
American brook lamprey (*Lampetra lamottei*)		✓	✓	✓		✓	✓	✓	✓	✓	✓	✓	✓
Sea lamprey (*Petromyzon marinus*)		✓	✓	✓		✓	✓		✓	✓			
Shortnose sturgeon (*Acipenser brevirostrum*)										✓			
Lake sturgeon (*A. fulvescens*)	✓	✓	✓	✓		✓	✓	✓	✓				
Atlantic sturgeon (*A. oxyrhynchus*)										✓			
Longnose gar (*Lepisosteus osseus*)	✓	✓	✓	✓		✓	✓	✓	✓				
Bowfin (*Amia calva*)		✓	✓	✓	✓	✓	✓	✓	✓				
American eel (*Anguilla rostrata*)		✓	✓	✓	✓	✓	✓		✓	✓	✓	✓	✓
Blueback herring (*Alosa aestivalis*)										✓			
Alewife (*A. pseudoharengus*)		✓								✓			✓

Distribution of New York Fishes (*Continued*)

SPECIES	DRAINAGES												
		Great Lakes–St. Lawrence											
	Allegheny	Erie	Ontario	Oswego	Genesee	St. Lawrence	Oswegatchie and Black	Raquette	Champlain	Hudson	Delaware	Susquehanna	Long Island
American shad (*A. sapidissima*)										✓	✓		✓
Gizzard shad (*Dorosoma cepedianum*)		✓	✓	✓									
Mooneye (*Hiodon tergisus*)	✓	✓	✓										
Cisco (*Coregonus artedii*)		✓	✓	✓	✓	✓	✓	✓	✓	✓			
Lake whitefish (*C. clupeaformis*)		✓	✓	✓	✓	✓	✓	✓	✓	✓		✓	
Bloater (*C. hoyi*)			✓										
Kiyi (*C. kiyi*)			✓										
Blackfin cisco (*C. nigripinnis*)			✓										
Shortnose cisco (*C. reighardi*)			✓										
Round whitefish (*Prosopium cylindraceum*)			✓			✓	✓	✓	✓	✓			
Coho salmon (*Oncorhynchus kisutch*)		✓	✓				✓						
Kokanee (*O. nerka*)									✓				
Chinook salmon (*O. tshawytscha*)		✓	✓										

Distribution of New York Fishes (*Continued*)

SPECIES		DRAINAGES												
	Allegheny	Great Lakes–St. Lawrence								Hudson	Delaware	Susquehanna	Long Island
		Erie	Ontario	Oswego	Genesee	St. Lawrence	Oswegatchie and Black	Raquette	Champlain				
Rainbow trout (*Salmo gairdneri*)	✓	✓	✓	✓	✓			✓	✓	✓		✓	✓
Atlantic salmon (*S. salar*)	✓	✓	✓			✓	✓	✓	✓	✓			
Brown trout (*S. trutta*)	✓	✓	✓	✓	✓	✓		✓	✓	✓	✓	✓	✓
Brook trout (*Salvelinus fontinalis*)		✓	✓	✓	✓	✓	✓	✓	✓	✓	✓	✓	✓
Lake trout (*S. namaycush*)		✓	✓	✓	✓		✓	✓	✓	✓	✓	✓	
Rainbow smelt (*Osmerus mordax*)			✓				✓	✓	✓	✓	✓		✓
Chain pickerel (*Esox niger*)		✓	✓	✓	✓		✓		✓	✓	✓	✓	✓
Redfin or grass pickerel (*E. americanus*)	✓	✓	✓				✓		✓	✓	✓		✓
Northern pike (*E. lucius*)	✓	✓	✓	✓	✓	✓	✓	✓	✓				
Muskellunge (*E. masquinongy*)	✓	✓	✓	✓	✓	✓			✓				
Central mudminnow (*Umbra limi*)	✓	✓								✓			
Eastern mudminnow (*U. pygmaea*)										✓			✓
Carp (*Cyprinus carpio*)	✓	✓	✓	✓	✓	✓	✓	✓	✓	✓		✓	✓

Distribution of New York Fishes (Continued)

SPECIES	Allegheny	Great Lakes–St. Lawrence								Hudson	Delaware	Susquehanna	Long Island
		Erie	Ontario	Oswego	Genesee	St. Lawrence	Oswegatchie and Black	Raquette	Champlain				
Goldfish (Carassius auratus)	🐟	🐟	🐟							🐟		🐟	🐟
Stoneroller (Campostoma anomalum)	🐟	🐟	🐟	🐟	🐟		🐟					🐟	
Golden shiner (Notemigonus crysoleucas)	🐟	🐟	🐟	🐟	🐟	🐟	🐟	🐟	🐟	🐟	🐟	🐟	🐟
Lake chub (Couesius plumbeus)			🐟	🐟		🐟			🐟	🐟	🐟		
Hornyhead chub (Nocomis biguttatus)		🐟	🐟	🐟	🐟					🐟		🐟	
River chub (N. micropogon)	🐟	🐟	🐟										
Bigeye chub (Hybopsis amblops)	🐟	🐟											
Silver chub (H. storeriana)		🐟											
Streamline chub (H. dissimilis)	🐟												
Cutlips minnow (Exoglossum maxillingua)			🐟	🐟	🐟	🐟	🐟	🐟	🐟	🐟	🐟	🐟	🐟
Tonguetied minnow (E. laurae)	🐟												
Redside dace (Clinostomus elongatus)	🐟	🐟	🐟	🐟	🐟					🐟		🐟	
Brassy minnow (Hybognathus hankinsoni)		🐟	🐟			🐟	🐟	🐟	🐟				

Distribution of New York Fishes (Continued)

SPECIES	DRAINAGES												
	Alle-gheny	Great Lakes–St. Lawrence								Hudson	Delaware	Susque-hanna	Long Island
		Erie	Ontario	Oswego	Genesee	St. Lawrence	Oswegatchie and Black	Raquette	Cham-plain				
Silvery minnow (H. nuchalis)		🐟	🐟	🐟	🐟				🐟	🐟	🐟	🐟	
Bridle shiner (Notropis bifrenatus)		🐟	🐟	🐟					🐟	🐟	🐟	🐟	
Swallowtail shiner (N. procne)				🐟					🐟		🐟	🐟	
Sand shiner (N. stramineus)		🐟	🐟		🐟	🐟	🐟						
Pugnose minnow (N. emiliae)		🐟											
Pugnose shiner (N. anogenus)	🐟	🐟		🐟	🐟		🐟		🐟	🐟			
Blacknose shiner (N. heterolepis)	🐟	🐟	🐟	🐟	🐟	🐟	🐟		🐟	🐟	🐟	🐟	
Spottail shiner (N. hudsonius)	🐟	🐟	🐟	🐟	🐟	🐟	🐟	🐟	🐟	🐟		🐟	
Spotfin shiner (N. spilopterus)	🐟	🐟	🐟		🐟	🐟	🐟		🐟	🐟		🐟	
Blackchin shiner (N. heterodon)	🐟	🐟	🐟	🐟	🐟	🐟	🐟		🐟	🐟		🐟	
Ironcolor shiner (N. chalybaeus)	🐟									🐟†	🐟		
Mimic shiner (N. volucellus)	🐟	🐟	🐟	🐟		🐟	🐟	🐟	🐟				

†Hackensack drainage only.

Distribution of New York Fishes (Continued)

SPECIES		DRAINAGES											
					Great Lakes–St. Lawrence								
	Allegheny	Erie	Ontario	Oswego	Genesee	St. Lawrence	Oswegatchie and Black	Raquette	Champlain	Hudson	Delaware	Susquehanna	Long Island
Bigmouth shiner (*N. dorsalis*)	🐟	🐟			🐟								
Satinfin shiner (*N. analostanus*)										🐟	🐟	🐟	
Common shiner (*N. cornutus*)	🐟	🐟	🐟	🐟	🐟		🐟		🐟	🐟	🐟	🐟	
Striped shiner (*N. chrysocephalus*)	🐟	🐟	🐟	🐟	🐟	🐟	🐟		🐟	🐟			
Redfin shiner (*Notropis umbratilis*)	🐟	🐟		🐟									
Emerald shiner (*N. atherinoides*)		🐟	🐟	🐟	🐟	🐟	🐟	🐟	🐟	🐟			
Silver shiner (*N. photogenis*)	🐟												
Rosyface shiner (*N. rubellus*)	🐟	🐟	🐟	🐟	🐟	🐟	🐟	🐟	🐟	🐟		🐟	
Comely shiner (*N. amoenus*)				🐟						🐟	🐟	🐟	
Steelcolor shiner (*N. whipplei*)		🐟		🐟									
Southern redbelly dace (*Phoxinus erythrogaster*)	🐟												
Finescale dace (*P. neogaeus*)						🐟	🐟	🐟	🐟	🐟			
Northern redbelly dace (*P. eos*)	🐟		🐟			🐟	🐟	🐟	🐟	🐟			

Distribution of New York Fishes (*Continued*)

Presence of a species in a drainage is indicated by ● (each ● represents a fish symbol in the original table).

DRAINAGES — columns Erie through Champlain are grouped under "Great Lakes–St. Lawrence."

SPECIES	Allegheny	Erie	Ontario	Oswego	Genesee	St. Lawrence	Oswegatchie and Black	Raquette	Champlain	Hudson	Delaware	Susquehanna	Long Island
Bluntnose minnow (*Pimephales notatus*)	●	●	●	●	●	●	●	●	●	●	●	●	
Fathead minnow (*P. promelas*)	●	●	●	●	●	●	●	●	●	●		●	
Blacknose dace (*Rhinichthys atratulus*)	●	●	●	●	●	●	●	●	●	●	●	●	
Longnose dace (*R. cataractae*)	●	●	●	●	●	●	●	●	●	●	●	●	
Rudd (*Scardinius erythrophthalmus*)										●			
Fallfish (*Semotilus corporalis*)	●	●	●	●		●	●	●	●	●	●	●	
Creek chub (*S. atromaculatus*)	●	●	●	●	●	●	●	●	●	●		●	
Pearl dace (*S. margarita*)	●	●	●	●	●	●	●	●	●	●		●	
Quillback (*Carpiodes cyprinus*)	●	●							●				
Longnose sucker (*Catostomus catostomus*)						●			●				
White sucker (*C. commersoni*)	●	●	●	●	●	●	●	●	●	●	●	●	●
Creek chubsucker (*Erimyzon oblongus*)			●	●	●		●	●		●	●	●	●
Lake chubsucker (*E. sucetta*)		●	●				●			●	●		

Distribution of New York Fishes (Continued)

SPECIES	DRAINAGES												
	Alle-gheny	Great Lakes–St. Lawrence								Hudson	Delaware	Susque-hanna	Long Island
		Erie	Ontario	Oswego	Genesee	St. Lawrence	Oswegatchie and Black	Raquette	Cham-plain				
Northern hog sucker (*Hypentelium nigricans*)	●	●	●	●	●					●		●	
Bigmouth buffalo (*Ictiobus cyprinellus*)		●											
Spotted sucker (*Minytrema melanops*)	●	●											
Silver redhorse (*Moxostoma anisurum*)	●	●	●	●		●		●	●				
River redhorse (*M. carinatum*)		●	●										
Golden redhorse (*M. erythrurum*)	●	●	●	●	●	●	●	●	●	●			
Shorthead redhorse (*M. macrolepidotum*)	●	●	●	●		●	●	●	●			●	
Greater redhorse (*M. valenciennesi*)	●	●	●			●			●	●			
Black redhorse (*M. duquesnei*)	●	●											
White catfish (*Ictalurus catus*)				●			●		●	●			
Channel catfish (*I. punctatus*)	●	●	●	●			●		●				
Yellow bullhead (*I. natalis*)	●	●	●	●						●			
Brown bullhead (*I. nebulosus*)	●	●	●	●	●	●		●	●	●	●	●	●

Distribution of New York Fishes *(Continued)*

SPECIES	Allegheny	Great Lakes–St. Lawrence								Hudson	Delaware	Susquehanna	Long Island
		Erie	Ontario	Oswego	Genesee	St. Lawrence	Oswegatchie and Black	Raquette	Champlain				
Black bullhead *(I. melas)*	●	●	●	●	●		●						
Stonecat *(Noturus flavus)*		●	●	●	●	●	●	●	●	●			
Tadpole madtom *(N. gyrinus)*		●	●	●	●		●			●	●		
Margined madtom *(N. insignis)*				●						●	●	●	
Brindled madtom *(N. miurus)*	●	●	●	●									
Pirate perch *(Aphredoderus sayanus)*													●
Trout perch *(Percopsis omiscomaycus)*	●	●		●	●	●	●	●	●	●		●	
Burbot *(Lota lota)*	●	●	●	●			●		●				
Atlantic tomcod *(Microgadus tomcod)*										●			
Sheepshead minnow *(Cyprinodon variegatus)*													●
Rainwater killifish *(Lucania parva)*													●
Banded killifish *(Fundulus diaphanus)*		●	●	●	●	●	●	●	●	●	●	●	●
Mummichog *(F. heteroclitus)*										●			●

Distribution of New York Fishes (Continued)

SPECIES	DRAINAGES												
	Allegheny	Great Lakes–St. Lawrence								Hudson	Delaware	Susquehanna	Long Island
		Erie	Ontario	Oswego	Genesee	St. Lawrence	Oswegatchie and Black	Raquette	Champlain				
Striped killifish (*F. majalis*)										✓*			✓
Spotfin killifish (*F. luciae*)										✓			✓
Brook silversides (*Labidesthes sicculus*)		✓	✓	✓	✓	✓	✓						
Tidewater silversides (*Menidia beryllina*)		✓	✓	✓	✓	✓	✓			✓		✓	✓
Brook stickleback (*Culaea inconstans*)		✓	✓	✓	✓	✓	✓	✓	✓	✓			
Threespine stickleback (*G. aculeatus*)		✓	✓	✓	✓	✓	✓			✓			
Fourspine stickleback (*Apeltes quadracus*)				✓			✓			✓			✓
Ninespine stickleback (*Pungitius pungitius*)			✓							✓*			✓
Fourhorn sculpin (*Myoxocephalus quadricornis*)			✓										
Mottled sculpin (*Cottus bairdi*)	✓	✓	✓	✓	✓	✓	✓	✓	✓	✓		✓	
Slimy sculpin (*C. cognatus*)	✓	✓	✓	✓	✓	✓	✓		✓	✓	✓	✓	
White perch (*Morone americana*)			✓	✓						✓			✓

*Tributaries into Long Island Sound only.

Distribution of New York Fishes (*Continued*)

SPECIES	Allegheny	Erie	Ontario	Oswego	Genesee	St. Lawrence	Oswegatchie and Black	Raquette	Champlain	Hudson	Delaware	Susquehanna	Long Island
		Great Lakes–St. Lawrence											
White bass (*M. chrysops*)	🐟	🐟	🐟	🐟						🐟			
Striped bass (*M. saxatilis*)										🐟			
Mud sunfish (*Acantharchus pomotis*)										🐟	🐟		🐟
Rock bass (*Ambloplites rupestris*)	🐟	🐟	🐟	🐟	🐟	🐟	🐟	🐟	🐟	🐟	🐟	🐟	🐟
Bluespotted sunfish (*Enneacanthus gloriosus*)				🐟						🐟†	🐟		🐟
Banded sunfish (*E. obesus*)										🐟‡	🐟		🐟
Redbreast sunfish (*Lepomis auritus*)						🐟	🐟	🐟	🐟	🐟	🐟	🐟	
Green sunfish (*L. cyanellus*)	🐟	🐟	🐟	🐟	🐟					🐟			
Pumpkinseed (*L. gibbosus*)	🐟	🐟	🐟	🐟	🐟	🐟	🐟	🐟	🐟	🐟	🐟	🐟	🐟
Warmouth (*L. gulosus*)		🐟	🐟	🐟									
Bluegill (*L. macrochirus*)	🐟	🐟	🐟	🐟	🐟	🐟	🐟		🐟	🐟	🐟	🐟	🐟
Longear sunfish (*L. megalotis*)		🐟	🐟	🐟									

Column group: **DRAINAGES**

†Hackensack drainage only.
‡Ramapo drainage only.

Distribution of New York Fishes (*Continued*)

SPECIES	Allegheny	Great Lakes–St. Lawrence								Hudson	Delaware	Susquehanna	Long Island
		Erie	Ontario	Oswego	Genesee	St. Lawrence	Oswegatchie and Black	Raquette	Champlain				
Smallmouth bass (*Micropterus dolomieui*)	🐟	🐟	🐟	🐟	🐟	🐟	🐟	🐟	🐟	🐟	🐟	🐟	🐟
Largemouth bass (*M. salmoides*)	🐟	🐟	🐟	🐟	🐟	🐟	🐟	🐟	🐟	🐟	🐟	🐟	🐟
White crappie (*Pomoxis annularis*)	🐟	🐟	🐟	🐟	🐟	🐟	🐟		🐟	🐟			🐟
Black crappie *P. nigromaculatus*)	🐟	🐟	🐟	🐟	🐟	🐟	🐟		🐟	🐟	🐟	🐟	🐟
Eastern sand darter (*Ammocrypta pellucida*)						🐟				🐟			
Greenside darter (*Etheostoma blennioides*)	🐟	🐟	🐟	🐟	🐟								
Rainbow darter (*E. caeruleum*)	🐟	🐟	🐟	🐟									
Iowa darter (*E. exile*)					🐟	🐟	🐟		🐟				
Fantail darter (*E. flabellare*)	🐟	🐟				🐟	🐟	🐟	🐟	🐟			
Swamp darter (*E. fusiforme*)												🐟	🐟
Spotted darter (*E. maculatum*)	🐟												
Johnny darter (*E. nigrum*)	🐟	🐟	🐟	🐟	🐟								
Tessellated darter (*E. olmstedi*)			🐟	🐟	🐟	🐟	🐟	🐟	🐟	🐟	🐟	🐟	🐟

Distribution of New York Fishes *(Continued)*

SPECIES		DRAINAGES												
	Allegheny	Great Lakes–St. Lawrence								Hudson	Delaware	Susquehanna	Long Island
		Erie	Ontario	Oswego	Genesee	St. Lawrence	Oswegatchie and Black	Raquette	Champlain				
Variegate darter *(E. variatum)*	✓												
Banded darter *(E. zonale)*	✓												
Logperch *(Percina caprodes)*	✓	✓	✓	✓	✓	✓	✓	✓	✓	✓			
Shield darter *(P. peltata)*										✓	✓	✓	
Channel darter *(P. copelandi)*		✓				✓	✓	✓	✓				
Gilt darter *(P. evides)*	✓												
Longhead darter *(P. macrocephala)*	✓	✓											
Blackside darter *(P. maculata)*	✓	✓	✓	✓	✓								
Yellow perch *(Perca flavescens)*	✓	✓	✓	✓	✓	✓	✓	✓	✓	✓	✓	✓	✓
Sauger *(Stizostedion canadense)*	✓	✓	✓	✓		✓			✓				
Walleye *(S. vitreum)*		✓	✓	✓	✓	✓	✓	✓	✓	✓	✓	✓	
Freshwater drum *(Aplodinotus grunniens)*		✓	✓	✓					✓				

organisms so that similar genera are grouped into one family, similar families are placed into an order, and similar orders are gathered into a class. This system assists in showing the relationships between fishes. When a number of families are discussed the normal procedure is to begin with the most primitive and end with the most advanced. We follow the same system in this guide.

How To Use This Book

MOST PEOPLE who work with fishes rely on a device, called a key, to assist them. A key will help lead to the correct identification of an unknown fish by pointing out the essential characteristics which separate one species from another.

After a fish has been identified, more can be learned about its life history and distribution by referring to the discussions that follow the keys. The life history of 68 of the most common species is presented. These species were chosen so that all of those most frequently encountered are included in the descriptions. Rare fish, or fish occupying remote habitats such as deep-water regions of Lake Ontario, are not described. Even so, a close relative of the rarer forms will more than likely be described.

The best approach when you have an unknown fish in hand is to first determine its family by going to the Key to Families (beginning on p. 33). Once you have done this, turn to the section of this book on that family and refer to the Species Key at the beginning of that section to find out which species you have. After you have identified your fish the odds are very good that your fish's life history is described and that additional references to the scientific literature are given. Whenever possible it is always good practice to double check an identification by comparing it to illustrations and by verifying that its distribution corresponds with its point of capture.

Fish Anatomy

In order to identify a fish you must know some basic facts about fish anatomy. Spend a few minutes here before going on to the keys. A look at Figures 2 and 3 and the accompanying discussion should help, too.

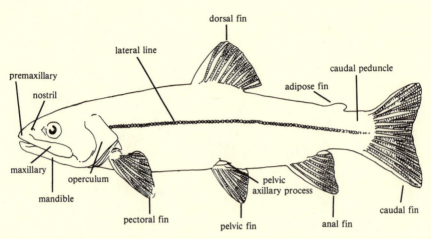

Figure 2. External anatomy of a typical soft-rayed fish

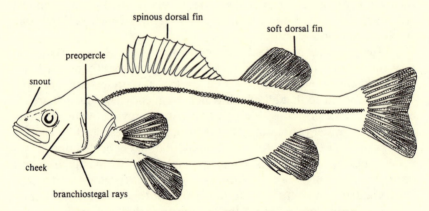

Figure 3. External anatomy of a typical spiny-rayed fish

Most fishes have three unpaired median fins and two sets of paired fins. The median unpaired fins are the dorsal, caudal, and anal fin. Some species also have an adipose fin, and others will have the dorsal composed of two or more parts. We shall look at each in turn.

The *dorsal fin* is located in the middle of the back, running fore and aft. It is simply a membrane supported by skeletal elements which, depending on the species, may be either spines, rays, or spinous rays. The type of element that supports the fin is quite important in identifying fishes. You will frequently have to distinguish spines from rays. Note in Figure 4 the unsegmented character of *spines*, the fact that they do not branch at the ends, and that they are of one solid piece when viewed from the front or back. A *soft ray* in contrast is segmented, quite often flares out at the end (branched), and appears to be split lengthwise when viewed from the front or back. A *spinous ray* is intermediate in that it is unbranched and quite massive, but it is divided lengthwise into two halves, and the segmentation is still present in the form of toothlike projections along its posterior (rear) edge. Spinous rays are found only in the carp, goldfish, and catfishes.

When counting rays in the minnow and sucker families, start the count from the forward edge of the fin with the first principal unbranched ray (Figure 5). This is the first full-length ray, just in front of the first branched ray. Ignore the short rudimentary rays that lie in front of the first principal ray, for they may vary in number. Then count every ray back through the fin until you reach the last two. If the two rays are joined at the base or are angled in such a way that it appears they will join shortly after they enter the body, count them as one ray. If, however, they appear to be separate and distinct, count them as two rays. When counting rays in the catfish, trout, or pike families, count all rudimentary rays.

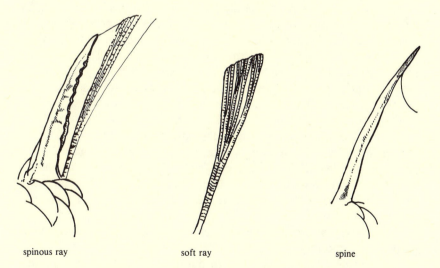

spinous ray   soft ray   spine

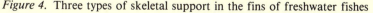

Figure 4. Three types of skeletal support in the fins of freshwater fishes

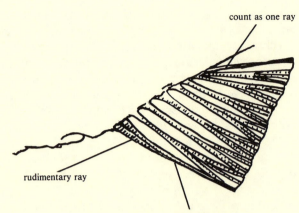

count as one ray

rudimentary ray

first principal unbranched ray

Figure 5. Method of counting rays of minnows and suckers. Begin count with the first principal unbranched ray, counting each ray to the end, unless the last two are joined. If so, count as one. The fish illustrated has 8 rays.

Between the dorsal fin and the caudal fin in trout, smelt, trout-perch, and catfish there is a small flap of tissue unsupported by spines or rays. This is the *adipose fin*.

The tail or, more properly, the *caudal fin* of fishes is supported by soft rays. Three types of caudal fins are found: heterocercal, abbreviate heterocercal, and homocercal. The *heterocercal caudal fin* has the vertebral column extending well into the upper lobe of the fin. The sturgeon is a fish with a well-developed heterocercal caudal fin (Figure 6). The *homocercal caudal fin* is distinguished in that the vertebral column does not enter the fin at all, but terminates at the base of the fin. Most fishes in New York possess this type of fin. The *abbreviate heterocercal* condition is intermediate and is found only in the bowfin and gar.

The *anal fin* is located on the ventral midline just behind the vent. There is only one anal fin in all of our freshwater species, with the exception of the brackish water tomcod which has two. The anal fin may have one or more spines at its leading edge, but the remainder of the fin is supported by soft rays.

The *pelvic fins* are paired and lie on either side of the midline. They are posterior and more ventral than the pectoral fins.

The *pectoral fins* are also paired, but are found farther up the side and more toward the head than the pelvic fins.

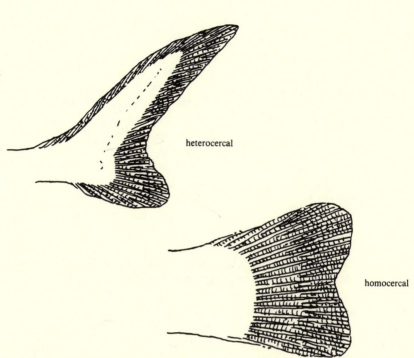

Figure 6. Heterocercal and homocercal caudal fin. Vertebral column extends into the upper lobe of the heterocercal fin, but it stops at the base of the fin in the homocercal condition.

The *head* of a fish extends from the tip of the snout to the posterior edge of the gill cover. The lower jaw is called the *mandible*. It is formed by the fusion of several bones, the major one being the dentary bone. On occasion, the lower jaw will possess holes on its ventral side called *mandibular pores*. Two bones form each half of the upper jaw, an anterior tooth-bearing bone called the *premaxilla* and a posterior bone called the *maxilla*. In some fishes the premaxillary bones are said to be *protractile*. This simply means that a distinct groove crosses all the way over the midline of the snout separating the premaxillary bones from the snout. If the premaxillary bones are nonprotractile, this groove will be bridged at the midline by a strip of flesh called a *frenum*.

Back on the snout a short way lie the *nostrils*. There are normally two pair — one pair on either side of the midline. Each generally has two openings separated by a fleshy flap. The eyes are set in a bony cavity called the *orbit*. The gills are protected by a flexible bony structure called the *operculum*. Anterior to the operculum is a narrow crescent-shaped bone called the *preoperculum*. Anterior to it is the *cheek region*. Ventral to the operculum is a membranous region which is supported by *branchiostegal rays*. By lifting the operculum you can see the *gills*. In most species there are 4 on either side of the head. The red feathery portion is composed of *gill filaments*. They are attached to a white bony *gill arch*. Protruding forward from the gill arch are small projections called *gill rakers*.

The teeth of fishes may be found in several places. In the upper jaw, teeth are found on the premaxilla. Moving toward the center of the oral cavity, the next teeth are the *palatine teeth*. Then on the midline near the front are the *vomerine teeth*. In the lower jaw teeth are found on the mandible, but they may also be found on the tongue and in some species pharyngeal tooth pads are present as well.

The body of most fishes is covered by scales. In the primitive fishes, sturgeon and gar, the scales are large, heavy and bony; but in most fish they will be thin, transparent, bony ridge scales. Two types of bony ridge scales occur in New York fishes — *cycloid scales* which are circular and relatively smooth, and *ctenoid scales* which possess small toothlike projections (ctenii) on the exposed portion of the scale.

Sometimes scales become specialized for certain purposes. Three cases of this are important in identifying fishes. In some species, just above the point where the pelvic fin joins the body, an enlarged pointed scale will appear. This is called the *pelvic axillary process*. A second special case occurs along the side of most fishes, where a faint line runs the length of the body from the head to the tail. At closer inspection you will note that the line is simply a series of holes in a row of scales. These scales are called *lateral line scales*. Of course, there are fish without scales which have lateral lines and also fish with scales that do not have lateral lines, but they are the exceptions. The third type of specialized scale is called a *scute*. It is a raised series of scales located on the ventral midline of the herrings, giving them a sawtooth appearance.

Internally the body cavity of fishes is lined by a thin membrane called a *peritoneum*.

Certain measurements are commonly made on fishes that are used in identification; they include:

Total length — the distance from the most anterior part of the head, either the tip of the snout or the end of the lower jaw, to the tip of the tail when the rays are squeezed together.

Standard length — the distance from the most anterior part of the head to the posterior tip of the vertebral column; the end of the vertebral column is determined by bending the tail until the crease formed can be discerned.

Fork length — the distance from the most anterior part of the head to the fork in the tail.

Body depth — measured as the vertical distance from the ventral midline to the dorsal midline; it is the greatest depth excluding fins.

Head length — the distance from the tip of the snout to the most posterior portion of the operculum.

Snout length — the distance from the tip of the snout to the most forward edge of the orbit or eye socket.

Length of upper jaw — the distance from the anterior edge of the premaxilla to the posterior edge of the maxilla.

Glossary

Abbreviate heterocercal: The condition in the tail fin of primitive fishes such as gars and bowfin where the vertebral column turns upwards, but only partially extends into the caudal fin; intermediate between homocercal and heterocercal.

Adipose eyelid: A pair of transparent membranes, one covering the anterior third of the eye, the other covering the posterior third of the eye; commonly found in the herring family.

Adipose fin: A small flap of fleshy tissue on the dorsal midline posterior to the dorsal fin. It is found in the catfish, trout, smelt, and troutperch families, among others.

Ammocoete: The larval stage of all lampreys.

Anadromous: Describes migration from the sea to fresh water for spawning, characteristic of salmon, lampreys, and herring, among others; the term is sometimes used when a landlocked species migrates from a large lake into a stream to spawn.

Anal fin: The fin located on the ventral midline of the body, usually just posterior to the vent.

Anterior: A relative position on the fish's body, anterior is more forward, toward the head.

Bicuspid: A tooth with two cusps or points.

Branchiostegal rays: A series of elongate bones extending fanlike from under the gill covers.

Buccal funnel: The oral chamber in lampreys, it lies anterior to the esophageal opening and is commonly lined with teeth.

Catadromous: Describes migration from fresh water to the sea to spawn, characteristic of the eel family.

Caudal fin: The tail fin of fishes.

Caudal peduncle: The part of the fish's body between the caudal fin base and the posterior portion of the anal fin.

Cheek: The portion of the side of the head which lies between the eye and the anterior edge of the gill cover.

Circumoral teeth: Teeth in the buccal funnel of lampreys which encircle the esophageal opening.

Complete lateral line: A condition that exists when the lateral line extends from the head to the tail in a regularly spaced series of pores.

Cycloid scales: Bony ridge scales that are smooth, largely circular, and lacking small spines or ctenii; characteristic of soft-rayed fishes.

Ctenoid scales: Bony ridge scales that possess small spines or ctenii on their exposed (posterior) margins; characteristic of spiny-rayed fishes.

Deciduous: A condition where a structure such as scales or teeth have a tendency to fall off at some stage of development.

Demersal eggs: Eggs that are heavier than water, with a sticky coating, and they sink and remain on the bottom.

Dentary bone: The major bone in the lower jaw, it normally contains the lower jaw teeth.

Dorsal: A relative position on the fish's body, dorsal is more toward the back or upper part of the body.

Dorsal fin: The fin located on the midline of the back between the head and tail; in some species more than one fin may be present.

Elvers: Young eels which are intermediate in development between the transparent leaflike larvae and the adult eels.

Family: A group of related fishes which form a taxonomic category above a genus and below an order.

Frenum: A membrane which connects the skin on the snout to the upper jaw, it is normally located on the midline.

Ganoid scales: Strong diamond-shaped scales with a hard enamel covering, found on gars.

Genital papilla: A small fleshy projection just posterior to the anal opening.

Gill arch: The skeletal element of the gill which contains the gill rakers and gill filaments. Located under the gill cover.

Head length: The greatest distance from the most anterior portion of the snout to the most posterior portion of the opercular membrane.

Heterocercal: A condition of the caudal fin where the vertebral column turns dorsally and enters the upper lobe of the caudal fin; found in sturgeons and paddlefish.

Homocercal: A condition of the caudal fin where the vertebral column ends in a flat bony plate and does not enter either lobe of the caudal fin; found in the vast majority of New York's fishes.

Incomplete lateral line: A lateral line that is either interrupted or does not extend all the way to the base of the caudal fin.

Inferior mouth: A mouth which is located on the underside of the head and often overhung by the snout, as in many suckers.

Isthmus: A narrow band of flesh (actually part of the breast) which lies between the gill covers on the ventral side and separates them; in some fishes the gill membranes are broadly connected to the isthmus, in others not.

Lateral line: A faint line running from the head region posteriorly to the base of the caudal fin. It is composed of canals and small pores.

Laterally compressed: Refers to a body shape which appears to have been compressed from both sides as in the sunfish.

Leptocephalus: The transparent leaflike larval stage of eels, a strictly marine stage in the life history of the eel.

Mandible: The lower jaw, which is composed primarily of the dentary bones.

Mandibular pores: Small openings on the ventral side of the mandible.

Maxilla: One of the bones in the upper jaw, the maxilla lies posterior and dorsal to the premaxilla and between them they comprise the upper jaw.

Median fins: Fins such as the dorsal, anal, and caudal fin which lie on the midline.

Myomeres: Blocks of muscle along the flanks of fishes which are divided by connective tissue; in adult fish they are most readily visible after the skin has been removed.

Nuptial tubercles: Small horny projections that appear on the head, body, and fins of some fishes during the breeding season; they are generally sloughed off after the breeding season is over; commonly appear in minnows and suckers.

Operculum: The thin flat bone that comprises the posterior portion of the gill cover.

Orbital rim: The bony socket which surrounds the eyeball.

Order: A group of related fishes which form a taxonomic category above a family and below a class.

Paired fins: Fins which are found on either side of the midline — the pelvic and pectoral fins.

Palatine teeth: Teeth rooted in the pair of palatine bones located in the roof of the mouth behind the median vomer.

Parr: Stage in the early life of a trout or salmon characterized by the presence of parr marks.

Parr marks: Dark rectangular markings on the sides of young trout and salmon.

Pectoral fin: The paired fins located along the side of the body, behind the head and anterior to the pelvic fins.

Pelagic: Pertaining to the open water habitat.

Pelvic axillary process: A small triangular flap of tissue located at the base of the pelvic fin.

Pelvic fin: The paired fins located near the ventral midline posterior to the pectoral fins.

Peritoneum: The thin membranous lining of the abdominal cavity.

Physoclistus: Refers to a fish possessing a gas bladder without a direct tubular connection to the alimentary canal.

Physostomous: Refers to a fish possessing a gas bladder with a direct connection to the alimentary canal; this connection is called a pneumatic duct.

Piscivorous: An adjective describing a predator which feeds on fishes.

Plicae: Ridges or folds of skin.

Posterior: A relative position on the fish's body, posterior is more toward the rear or tail region.

Premaxilla: The bone which forms the portion of the upper jaw that is most anterior and medial, it normally bears teeth.

Preoperculum: One of the thin flat bones comprising the gill cover, it lies anterior to the operculum and behind the eye.

Principal unbranched ray: A ray which is not branched, but is fully developed and reaches to the outer edge of the fin.

Radii: Markings on a fish scale which radiate outward from the central focus of the scale.

Ray or soft ray: A segmented, paired, generally branched supporting element in the fins of fishes.

Redd: The gravelly nest of a trout or salmon formed by the digging and covering movements of the female prior to and just after spawning.

Scute: Pointed scales that protrude from the body in a row along the ventral midline of herrings, they give a sawlike edge to the belly of herrings.

Spine: An unsegmented, unpaired generally stiff supporting element in the fins of many fishes which is pointed at its distal end.

Spinous ray: A soft ray which has become hardened and is not branched; segmentation may be retained in the form of serrations on its posterior edge, found in carp, goldfish, and catfish.

Spiracle: An opening from the outside into the mouth cavity, located dorsal and posterior to the eye.

Subterminal mouth: A mouth whose position is intermediate between terminal (at the most anterior end) and inferior (ventrally located), it is normally just slightly more ventral than a terminal mouth.

Terminal mouth: A mouth whose position is at the most anterior end of the fish.

Unicuspid: A tooth with a single cusp or point.

Vent: The opening of the intestine to the outside; anus.

Ventral: A relative position on the fish's body, ventral is more toward the underneath side or belly region of the fish.

Viscera: Internal organs.

Vomerine teeth: Teeth located on the vomerine bone, found in the roof of the mouth on the midline, just posterior to the upper jaw bones.

Using the Key

The Key to Families is designed to assist you in identifying a fish. Since identifying fish often requires careful observation of characteristics it is best to have the specimen in hand. Occasionally you can make a positive identification of a fish in the water with the aid of illustrations, much as you might do with birds, but more often than not the fish will present you with a limited view of short duration. Thus, whenever possible, obtain a specimen. It can be examined fresh or, if necessary, preserved in 10 percent formalin.

The keys in this book are called dichotomous keys because you are asked to choose between two alternatives. Once you have made your choice the number on the right-hand side of the page directly opposite the chosen alternative will tell you where to go next. Follow the numbers, making the appropriate choice at each dichotomy until you find a name. In the Key to Families this will be the name of the family of your specimen. You can verify the identification by comparing your specimen with the illustration.

For example, suppose you have an American eel in hand, but you do not know what it is. First go to dichotomy 1 in the Key to Families. Read both 1a and 1b. Since your fish has jaws, pectoral fins, one gill opening on each side, and a pair of nostrils, you would choose 1b and be instructed to go to dichotomy 2. There you will decide whether the dorsal or upper lobe of the caudal fin is larger than the ventral or lower lobe. Since it is not, you then go to dichotomy 3. Here you are asked whether the ventral surface of the lower jaw is protected by a flat bony plate. It is not, so you go to dichotomy 4, where you must decide whether the snout of your fish is greatly elongated. Since the snout is of normal length you are led to dichotomy 5. Here you must decide whether the fish has pelvic fins or not. It does not, and you will also note that its body is eel shaped. This leads to the conclusion that your specimen is in the eel family, Anguillidae. Verify this by comparing it with the drawing at 5a. If by chance the drawing and the specimen do not agree, go back and run through the key again, rechecking your choices.

Once you have determined the family, you should look it up in the Description of New York's Freshwater Fishes. Once again run through the key to species just as you did in the Key to Families and determine the exact identification. In our example there is only one species of eel in New York, *Anguilla rostrata*, the American eel.

Key to Families

1a. Mouth a round sucking disc, no jaws; no pelvic or pectoral fins; 7 porelike gill openings on either side of head; single median nostril . . . . Lamprey, Family Petromyzontidae

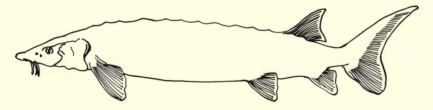

1b. Mouth with true jaws; pectoral fins always present, pelvic fins present in all families save the eels; one large slit-like gill opening on either side of head; pair of nostrils on snout 2

2a. Dorsal lobe of caudal fin much larger than ventral lobe . . . .
Sturgeon, Family Acipenseridae

2b. Both lobes of caudal fin of approximately the same size 3

3a. Ventral surface of lower jaw protected by a flat bony plate; long dorsal fin with more than 45 soft rays and extending over half the length of the body .... Bowfin, Family Amiidae

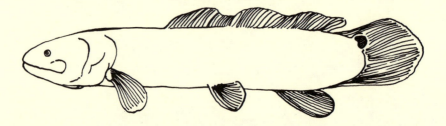

3b. Ventral surface of lower jaw fleshy, protected only by mandibular bones; dorsal fin either long or short 4

4a. Snout greatly elongate comprising at least 20 percent of total length; body covered with heavy diamond-shaped ganoid scales .... Gar, Family Lepisosteidae

4b. Snout of normal length; body with normal scales or scaleless 5

5a. Pelvic fins absent; dorsal, caudal and anal fins joined to form single fin; body eel shaped .... Eel, Family Anguillidae

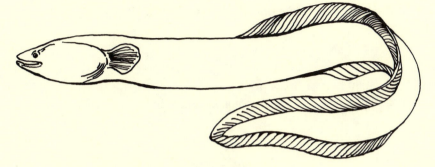

5b. Pelvic fins present; dorsal, caudal, and anal fins usually
    separate 6

6a. Adipose fin present.......................................7

6b. Adipose fin absent 10

7a. 4–8 barbels surrounding mouth; no scales .... Catfish,
                                            Family Ictaluridae

7b. No barbels around mouth; scales present....................8

8a. A small flap of tissue present at base of pelvic fin (pelvic axillary process) .... Trout and whitefish, Family Salmonidae

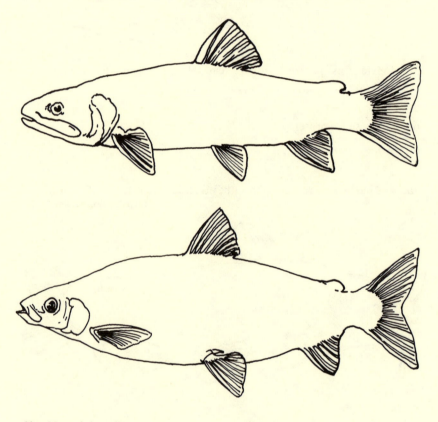

8b. No pelvic axillary process 9

9a. Body covered with ctenoid scales that feel rough when rubbed from the rear forward; pectoral fin extends well backward beyond base of pelvic fin....... Troutperch, Family Percopsidae

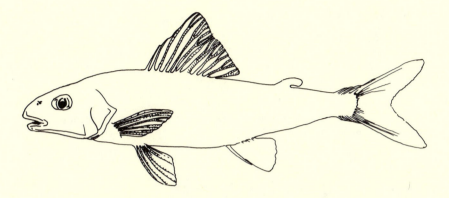

9b. Body covered with cycloid scales that feel smooth when rubbed;
tip of pectoral fin does not reach back to base of pelvic fin
.... Smelt, Family Osmeridae

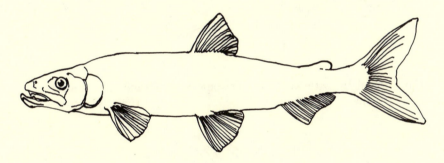

10a. A single barbel located at the tip of the lower jaw ..... Burbot,
Family Gadidae

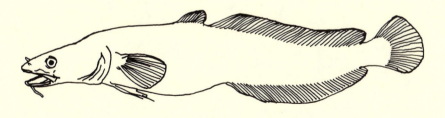

10b. No barbel at tip of lower jaw................................11

12a. Dorsal fin with 2–10 stout spines, membrane connects spines to
back, not to adjacent spine .... Stickleback,
Family Gasterosteidae

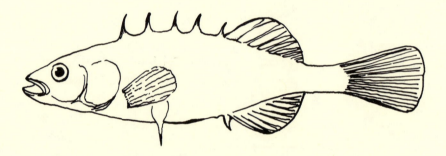

12b. Dorsal fin with weak slender spines, membrane interconnects
all spines one to the other .... Sculpin, Family Cottidae

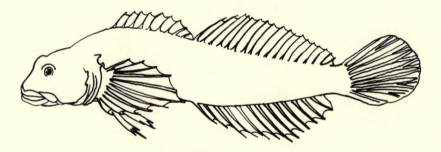

14a. Base of dorsal fin located, in part, directly over base of anal fin; lateral line complete; belly without sawtooth edge down midline.....................Mooneye, Family Hiodontidae

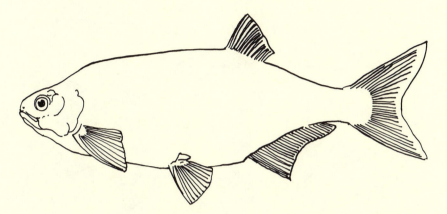

14b. Base of dorsal fin located over pelvic fin base, not over anal fin base; no lateral line; belly with row of specialized scales (scutes) down midline, forming a sawtooth edge .... Alewife,
Family Clupeidae

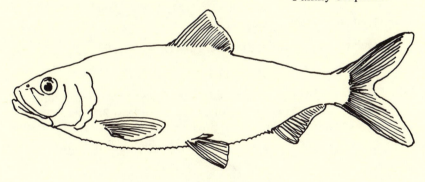

15a. Either a single dorsal fin composed entirely of segmented soft rays, or a single dorsal fin with one stout serrated spine at anterior edge followed by soft rays 16

15b. Either 2 distinctly separated dorsal fins; or, if dorsal fins are continuous, the anterior portion contains 2 or more unsegmented spines 21

16a. A large stout spine with double serrations on posterior edge at forward edge of dorsal fin .... Carp and goldfish,
Family Cyprinidae (in part)

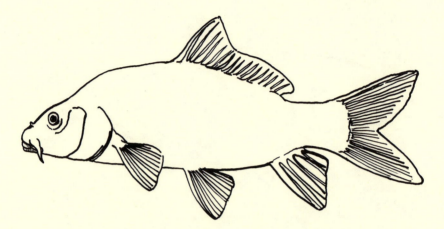

16b. A single dorsal fin composed entirely of segmented soft rays 17

17a. Head completely scaleless 18
17b. Head with some scales; the cheeks always with scales...........19

18a. Dorsal rays 10 or more; anal fin set far posterior, distance from base of first anal ray to base of caudal fin at least 2.5 times distance from front of anal fin to tip of snout (see Figure 7) ......
Sucker, Family Catostomidae

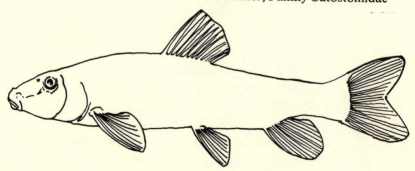

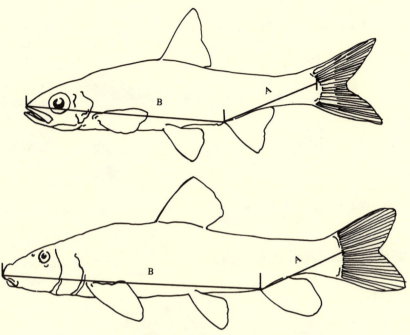

Figure 7. Method of distinguishing minnows from suckers using the position of the anal fin. In suckers the distance A goes into the distance B at least 2.5 times; for minnows A goes into B fewer than 2.5 times.

18b. Dorsal rays usually 8; anal fin set more anterior, distance from base of first anal ray to base of caudal fin contained less than 2.5 times in distance from front of anal fin to tip of snout . . . . .
Minnow, Family Cyprinidae (in part)

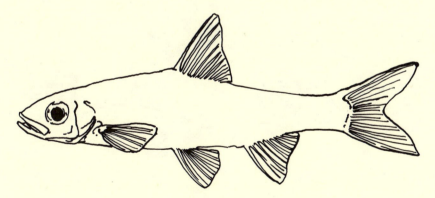

19a. Tail forked; jaws forming a ducklike snout . . . . Pike,
Family Esocidae

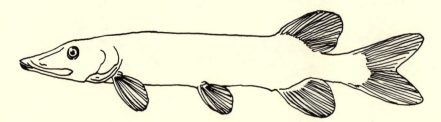

19b. Tail rounded; jaws shorter and not forming a ducklike snout 20

20a. Premaxillaries not protractile . . . . Mudminnow,
Family Umbridae

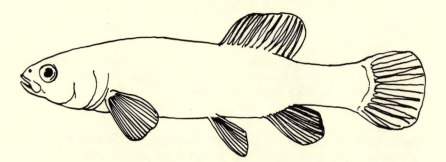

20b. Premaxillaries protractile . . . Killifish, Family Cyprinodontidae

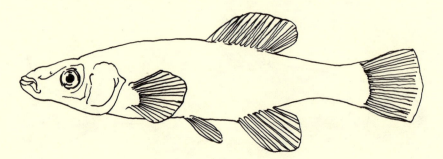

21a. 2 separate and distinguishable dorsal fins 22

21b. Dorsal fins completely joined; may be notched, but never completely separated 24

22a. Anal fin base much longer than dorsal fin bases......Silverside,
Family Atherinidae

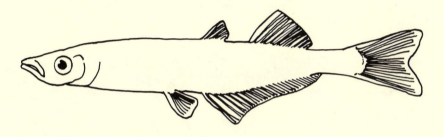

22b. Anal fin base shorter than dorsal fin bases...................23

23a. Anal spines 3.........Temperate bass, Family Percichthyidae

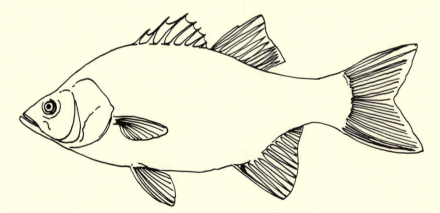

23b. Anal spines 1 or 2 . . . . Perch, Family Percidae

24a. Anus located on throat, anterior to pectoral fins in adults . . . . .
Pirate perch, Family Aphredoderidae

24b. Anus in normal position, posterior to pectoral fins 25

25a. Anal spines 2; lateral line extending onto caudal fin . . . . Drum,
Family Sciaenidae

25b. Anal spines 3 or more; lateral line does not extend onto caudal fin........................Sunfish, Family Centrarchidae

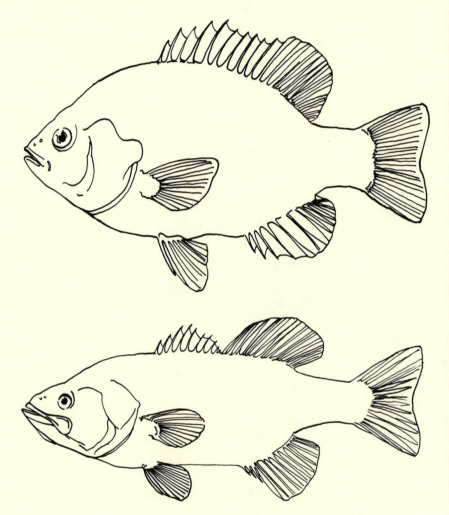

Description of New York's Freshwater Fishes

Lamprey   Family Petromyzontidae

THE LAMPREYS are the most primitive fishes in New York waters. Their skeleton is composed entirely of cartilage; they have no lower jaw and just a single nasal opening. Their life cycle typically involves one to 5 years as a filter-feeding larva (ammocoetes) followed by 1–18 months as a free–swimming adult. Some species are parasitic on other fishes, but many are quite harmless.

Thirty-one species of lamprey are known for the world, of which 5 live in New York. The most common and certainly the most significant economically is the sea lamprey, *Petromyzon marinus*.

SPECIES KEY (Adults Only)

1a. Dorsal fin divided into 2 separate distinguishable fins 2

1b. Dorsal fin not divided, one continuous fin, though it may be notched 3

2a. Large, pointed teeth radiating outward in a series, spawning adults 13–30 inches long, parasitic .... sea lamprey, *Petromyzon marinus*

2b. Small blunt, inconspicuous teeth in clusters, spawning adults 5–8 inches long, nonparasitic .... American brook lamprey, *Lampetra lamottei*

3a. Circumoral teeth (inner teeth forming circle around mouth) unicuspid; myomeres (muscle segments) fewer than 55 from last gill opening to anus 4

3b. Circumoral teeth bicuspid; myomeres more than 55 from last gill opening to anus; nonparasitic . . . . Allegheny brook lamprey, *Ichthyomyzon greeleyi*

4a. Large sharply pointed teeth; spawning adults 10–14 inches; parasitic . . . . silver lamprey, *Ichthyomyzon unicuspis*

4b. Small, blunt, partially hidden teeth, spawning adults 5–7 inches; nonparasitic . . . . northern brook lamprey, *Ichthyomyzon fossor*

Sea Lamprey   *Petromyzon marinus* Linnaeus

Identification

All lampreys have a sucking disc in place of movable jaws and resemble eels in the shape of their body. The sea lamprey has 2 separate and distinct dorsal fins and an impressive array of teeth in its buccal funnel which radiate out in all directions from the mouth. The only other lamprey in the state with 2 dorsal fins is the American brook lamprey. It is a smaller fish and can be distinguished from the sea lamprey by the fact that its teeth are clustered in groups instead of radiating out from the mouth. Other lampreys that may be found in New York are in the genus *Ichthyomyzon* and will all have a single dorsal fin. One, the Allegheny brook lamprey (*I. greeleyi*) has bicuspid teeth; while the teeth of the silver lamprey (*I. unicuspis*) and northern brook lamprey (*I. fossor*) are unicuspid. The silver lamprey is parasitic on fishes and thus has sharply pointed teeth, whereas the northern brook lamprey is nonparasitic and has blunt teeth.

Before they begin their spawning run, adult sea lamprey are generally tan with blotches of darker brown scattered across the body. During the spawning run they become bluish-black dorsally with a lighter-colored belly.

Life History

Adult sea lampreys move into streams in the spring, usually in May, to spawn. The male normally arrives first and creates a small depression in the gravelly stream bottom by attaching his sucker mouth to stones and displacing them. Sites chosen for nests are usually in shallow, swiftly flowing stretches of the stream. When the female arrives and the nest is finished the male attaches himself to the female, wraps his body around her, and eggs and sperm are simultaneously released into the gravel-bottomed nest. A single female has been known to produce as many as 235,000 eggs. After spawning the adults die.

The young hatch and leave the nest in a few days, drifting downstream until they settle into the soft mud on the bottom. They burrow into the mud and feed on organic material that washes to them. During this time, they are called ammocoetes and are quite harmless; in fact, the ammocoete is occasionally used for bait. Ammocoetes grow for about 5 years before transforming into adults.

Upon transformation the sea lamprey migrates downstream to the ocean (or lake if landlocked) and begins a parasitic existence. It feeds by attaching itself to other fish, using the teeth on its tongue to rasp a hole in the fish's side and consume its blood and body tissues. To facilitate feeding, an anti-coagulant is secreted by the lamprey. After 1–1½ years in the parasitic phase the adults achieve sexual maturity and migrate upstream to spawn and die.

The sea lamprey has earned a bad reputation as a severe predator on desirable sport fishes. Anglers frequently notice nasty-looking scars on the sides of fish they catch. While some of this reputation is certainly deserved, the presence of scars on otherwise healthy fish indicates that a single attack by a lamprey is not necessarily sufficient to kill a robust fish. In fact, lake trout have been taken with as many as 10 scars. A part of the lamprey's reputation is surely derived from its lack of beauty and unappealing mode of life.

A lamprey control program was initiated on Lake Ontario in 1972 by New York State and in 1971 by Canada. A selective poison was placed in the tributary streams known to contain lampreys to kill the ammocoetes. This has resulted in a decline in lamprey abundance in Lake Ontario.

Distribution

Sea lampreys are marine fish that spawn in fresh water. Some have become landlocked in our large inland lakes. They are found on both sides of the Atlantic from Greenland and Norway south to Florida and Africa. In New York they are known from Lake Ontario and Lake Erie, and Seneca, Cayuga, Champlain, and Oneida Lakes. Spawning adults and ammocoetes are found in small coastal streams as well as larger rivers, such as the Delaware, St. Lawrence, Hudson, and Susquehanna.

Other Name

Lamprey eel

Selected Lamprey References

Gage, S. H. 1928. "The Lampreys of New York State—Life History and Economics." In *A Biological Survey of the Oswego River System.* Suppl. 17th Ann. Rep. N.Y. Conserv. Dept. pp. 158–91.

Hardisty, M. W., and I. C. Potter, eds. 1971. *The Biology of the Lampreys.* New York: Academic.

Lawrie, A. H. 1970. "The Sea Lamprey in the Great Lakes." *Trans. Amer. Fish Soc.* 99(4):766–75.

Lennon, R. E. 1954. "Feeding Mechanism of the Sea Lamprey and its Effect on Host Fishes." *U.S. Fish Wildlife Serv. Fish Bull.* 98, vol. 56: 247–93.

Surface, A. H. 1898. "The Lampreys of Central New York." *Ext. U.S. Fish Comm. Bull.* 1897, vol. 17: 209–15.

Wigley, R. L. 1959. "Life History of the Sea Lamprey of Cayuga Lake, New York." *U.S. Fish Wildlife Serv. Fish Bull.* 154, vol. 59: 561–617.

Sturgeon   **Family Acipenseridae**

The sturgeons are very large, long-lived fishes of lakes and large rivers. They have long snouts with a ventral mouth preceded by 4 barbels, spiracles, and no teeth. The body is protected by 5 rows of large bony plates, one dorsal, 2 lateral, and 2 ventral. The tail is heterocercal; that is, the vertebral column extends into the upper lobe of the caudal fin.

World wide, 23 species are known, with 3 found in New York.

SPECIES KEY

1a. Width of mouth is less than 55 percent of the distance between eye sockets; 17–27 gill rakers; postdorsal and preanal shields paired; viscera light colored; primarily marine, occasionally enters freshwater stretches of the Hudson River . . . .
Atlantic sturgeon, *Acipenser oxyrhynchus*

1b. Width of mouth greater than 62 percent of the distance between eye sockets; 22–40 gill rakers; postdorsal and preanal shields in a single row; black viscera; fresh or brackish water species 2

2a. Gill rakers 22–29; 8–13 dorsal shields; 25–32 lateral shields; generally less than 40 inches long; an endangered species of the Hudson River .... shortnose sturgeon, *Acipenser brevirostrum*

2b. Gill rakers 25–40; 9–17 dorsal shields; 29–42 lateral shields; commonly more than 40 inches long; fresh water ....
lake sturgeon, *Acipenser fulvescens*

Lake Sturgeon   *Acipenser fulvescens* Rafinesque

Identification

The sturgeons are readily distinguished from other fishes in that their vertebral column extends well into the upper lobe of their forked caudal fin and by the 5 rows of large plate-like scales on their bodies. The lake sturgeon is the most common sturgeon in New York, but there are 2 other species known from the Hudson River which may be locally abundant in certain areas. These are the shortnose sturgeon, *Acipenser brevirostrum*, and the Atlantic sturgeon, *Acipenser oxyrhynchus*. The lake sturgeon has not been reported from the Hudson River. The lake sturgeon is olive green on the back, gray on the sides, and light gray to white on the belly.

Life History

Sturgeons spawn in May or June, in large rivers. They prefer stone or sand bottoms for the deposition of eggs. Spawning has never been observed, but it is not uncommon to see large sturgeon leaping out of the water during this time of the year, a behavior which may be associated with spawning. Females, depending on size, carry from 180,000 to 680,000 eggs, and spawn once every 4 or 5 years after reaching maturity at about age 12. Males may spawn more frequently.

Lake sturgeon are quite long-lived fish; reliable reports exist of individuals 50 years old. They grow throughout their life, even though the growth rate slows down after sexual maturity. In the St. Lawrence River fish weighing more than 80 pounds and measuring more than 5½ feet in length have been reported. In Canada, an individual weighing 275 pounds was reported. The normal size, however, is considerably smaller than this.

Lake sturgeon occur only in large bodies of water and generally stay close to the bottom. They overwinter in deep, well-oxygenated holes. They feed on a variety of bottom organisms, including insects, worms, molluscs, and crustaceans. The barbels around their mouths help them to locate food, which they pick up rapidly. Mud and dirt accompanying the food is expelled through the gill openings.

A small commercial fishery for lake sturgeon exists in Lake Ontario and the St. Lawrence River. The flesh is quite tasty, particularly when smoked, and the eggs or roe are sold in the gourmet section of the market as caviar. The sturgeon is not considered a sport fish by many anglers in New York, yet it can be taken on a hook and line by fishing near the bottom with nightcrawlers or cut bait.

Distribution

The lake sturgeon is found in large lakes and rivers from the Hudson Bay region of Canada southward down the Mississippi Valley to Alabama. In New York it is found in the Great Lakes–St. Lawrence drainage.

Other Names

Common sturgeon, rock sturgeon, Great Lakes sturgeon, smoothback

Selected Sturgeon References

Dees, L. T. 1961. "Sturgeons." U.S. Fish Wildlife Serv. Fish. Leafl. 526: 8 p.

Harkness, W. J. K. 1923. "The Rate of Growth and the Food of the Lake Sturgeon (*Acipenser rubicundus* LeSueur)." *Univ. Toronto Stud. Biol.* Ser. 18, Publ. Ont. Fish. Res. Lab. 18: 15–42.

Harkness, W. J. K., and J. R. Dymond. 1961. "The Lake Sturgeon. The History of its Fishery and Problems of Conservation." *Ont. Dept. Lands Forests, Fish Wildlife Br.*

Vladykov, V. D., and J. R. Greeley. 1963. "Order Acipenseroidei." *Fishes of the Western North Atlantic.* Mem. Sears Found. Mar. Res. 1(3):24–60.

Gar   Family Lepisosteidae

The gar is a slender cylindrical fish, well protected with heavy diamond-shaped ganoid scales. It has a long snout with the nasal sacs at the tip, and a jaw full of teeth making it a very effective predator. The vertebral column extends into the upper lobe of the caudal fin. In the young gar this is quite conspicuous. In older fish the vertebral column is hidden and the caudal fin appears symmetrical. The gas bladder is connected to the gut and is used as an accessory breathing organ.

Only 7 species are known worldwide, of which only one, the longnose gar, is found in New York.

| Longnose Gar | *Lepisosteus osseus* (Linnaeus) |

Identification

Gar are easily identified by the long bony snout and the heavy diamond-shaped ganoid scales. Only the longnose gar is found in New York.

The longnose gar is bluish-green on its back, shading to a cream color on its belly. The fins are yellow-orange with large black spots.

Life History

Longnose gar gather in shallow water in late May or early June. Spawning occurs in groups composed of one female and several males. The adhesive eggs are broadcast across the bottom, hatching in 3–9 days. The larvae remain attached to objects in their environment by means of a sucker on the ventral side of their snout until their yolk sac is absorbed. The young gar feed on small crustaceans and insect larvae until they are about two inches long. They then switch to small fish as their primary source of food. It takes 3–6 years for gar to reach sexual maturity, and they may live for as long as 22 years. A 2½-foot female carries about 12,000 eggs, which are green and poisonous. Gar will grow up to 4 feet long, but most individuals are about 2½ feet long and weigh around 2 pounds.

Longnose gar are commonly found close to shore in weedy lakes or rivers. They swim or float rather sluggishly near the surface, usually in groups of 3–12 individuals, and are often mistaken for floating logs by the casual observer. When feeding, however, they can move rapidly to capture their favorite prey — small fish.

There is no significant fishery for gar even though, with experience, they can be taken on hook and line using minnows and a wire leader. Occasionally, gar are speared from a lighted boat at night. In Chautauqua Lake and Lake Champlain a special fishery for gar has developed. The fish are stalked by boat with a man standing in the front armed with bow and arrow.

Distribution

Longnose gar range from the Dakotas to Quebec and south to Florida and northern Mexico. In New York they are found in the Great Lakes and St. Lawrence River, Lake Champlain, Chautauqua Lake, and the Oswego, Seneca and Niagara Rivers.

Other Names

Gar, gar-pike, bill-fish, needlenose

Selected Gar References

Netsch, Lt. Norval F., and A. Witt, Jr. 1962. "Contributions to the Life History of the Longnose Gar *(Lepisosteus osseus)* in Missouri." *Trans. Amer. Fish. Soc.* 91(3): 251–62.

Suttkus, R. D. 1963. "Order Lepisostei." *Fishes of the western North Atlantic. Mem. Sears Found. Mar. Res.* 1(3): 61–88.

Bowfin   Family Amiidae

The bowfin is a stocky fish, somewhat like the black basses, with a flat bony plate (median gular plate) on the underside of its lower jaw. Its caudal fin is abbreviate heterocercal. The gas bladder is connected to the gut and gives the bowfin a limited capability of breathing air.

Only one species of this family is known, and it is found in the fresh waters of eastern North America. The family forms a link between the gar and such primitive teleosts as herring and trout.

Bowfin   *Amia calva* Linnaeus

Identification

The bowfin is the only extant member of this ancient family of fishes. It has a very long uniform dorsal fin that extends over most of the length of the back and contains more than 45 soft rays. It is dark olive green on its back and head, grading to a pale yellow on its underside. At the dorsal side of the base of the caudal fin a dark spot is present, which is very conspicuous in males, less so in females.

Life History

Some time in May or June the male bowfin enters shallow weedy areas and begins to construct a nest. He clears out the vegetation by biting and pushing with his head, fins, and body until he has created a circular depression 4–8 inches deep and 1½–2½ feet in diameter. In a day or two, after dark, his nest will be visited by a female. They will mate and leave several thousand fertilized eggs in the nest. The female may repeat this process at other nests, and the male may be visited by more than one female. A nest will normally contain 2,000–5,000 eggs. The eggs hatch in eight to ten days, and the young larvae attach themselves to the roots and pebbles at the bottom of the nest by an adhesive organ on their snouts. They remain in the nest for another 7–9 days before they become free swimming and leave the nest in a tightly packed school. During the period of time that the young are in the nest and swimming in a tight school the male actively guards them. He normally rests in a tunnel formed by pushing through the thick vegetation with his head resting at the edge of the nest. If an intruder appears he is viciously attacked.

Bowfin are long-lived fish, some having been kept in captivity up to 30 years. The average bowfin weighs 2½–3½ pounds and measures 1½–2 feet in length, although some individuals have been reported which were 28 inches long and weighed 8.7 pounds.

They live in weedy, clear lakes and sluggish rivers, usually in shallow water. They feed very heavily on fish and crayfish and for this reason are thought to be undesirable. They may, however, play a beneficial role by controlling populations of panfish, which have a tendency to stunt when they become too abundant.

Little intentional effort is made to capture bowfin for commercial or sporting purposes in New York. A few fortunate fishermen have discovered the fighting qualities of the bowfin, and this angling sport may grow. It can be taken on live bait or plugs and will put up a good fight, quite like that of a largemouth bass.

Distribution

Bowfin are found throughout the United States from the Mississippi River east. They range from southern Canada to Florida. In New York they are found in the Great Lakes and St. Lawrence River, Lakes Champlain, Cayuga, Neahtawanta, and Oneida, as well as the Raquette and Seneca Rivers.

Other Names

Dogfish, grindle, lawyer, scaled ling

Selected Bowfin References

Lagler, K. F., and C. L. Hubbs. 1940. "Food of the Long-nosed Gar *(Lepisosteus osseus oxyurus)* and the Bowfin *(Amia calva)* in Southern Michigan." *Copeia* 1940(4): 239–41.

Reighard, J. E. 1904. *The Natural History of* Amia calva *Linnaeus, No. 4.* New York: Henry Holt, pp. 57–109.

Eel   Family Anguillidae

The eel is characterized by an elongated body, no pelvic fins, a pneumatic duct leading to the gas bladder, soft-rayed fins, and an elongate skull.

Approximately 15 species of eels are found in the world. Only one, *Anguilla rostrata*, is found in New York.

American Eel   *Anguilla rostrata* (LeSueur)

Identification

The eel is easily distinguished by the elongated shape of its body and should not be confused with any other species. The only fish bearing any resemblance to the eel is the lamprey, which also has an elongate body. Since lampreys have no jaws, 7 pairs of pore-like gill openings, and no pectoral fins, whereas the eel has jaws, pectoral fins, and a single pair of gill slits, the confusion should be slight. The color of the eel changes with its stages of development. For most of its life in fresh water it is yellow-brown to olive-brown in color with the back darker and the belly lighter. As it reaches sexual maturity the back becomes almost black while the belly changes to a silvery color.

Life History

The eel has an extremely interesting life history. It is the only fish in New York which undertakes a catadromous migration. Early in the spring the mature fish, which have been living in fresh water, begin to migrate downstream at night toward the ocean. Upon reaching the ocean they migrate to the Sargasso Sea, where they spawn and presumably die. The eggs drift back northward with the current, eventually hatching into transparent ribbonlike larvae called leptocephali. After about a year the leptocephali transform into small eel-like fish called elvers. They migrate up the Delaware, Hudson, St. Lawrence, and other coastal streams. The young eels then feed and grow for 5 to 20 years until they reach sexual maturity and return to the Sargasso Sea. Females are generally larger than males, sometimes reaching a length of 6 feet, but more commonly 3 feet. Eels are very effective carnivores, feeding heavily at night on a variety of prey organisms including fish.

Eels are an excellent food fish, and consequently a commercial fishery for eel has developed in New York State. In Lake Ontario, 25–50,000 pounds are landed annually. In the lower Hudson and Delaware Rivers 125–150,000 pounds are caught each year. Eels are also taken while bait fishing, and even though they are not the most exciting fish to catch, keep in mind their good eating qualities. Eels can be fried, broiled, baked, chopped up into soups or chowders, and smoked.

Distribution

The eel is found in streams and lakes along the eastern coast of North America from Labrador south to the West Indies and including the coast of the Gulf of Mexico. In New York it is found in all of the major drainages including those on Long Island.

Other Names

Eel, common eel, freshwater eel, silver eel

Selected Eel References

Bertin, L. 1956. *The World of Eels. Eels, A Biological Study*. London: Cleaver-Hume Press.

Schmidt, J. 1925. "The Breeding Places of the Eel." *Ann. Rep. Smithson. Inst.* 1924: 279–316.

Herring   Family Clupeidae

Herring are slender, laterally compressed, physostomous fishes with scutes along the ventral midline. They have no lateral line or adipose fin. The eyes are furnished with an adipose eyelid.

Most of the 180 species of herring are marine. Three species in 2 genera are found in fresh water in New York. They are the American shad (*Alosa sapidissima*), alewife (*Alosa pseudoharengus*), and gizzard shad (*Dorosoma cepedianum*). A fourth species, the blueback herring (*Alosa aestivalis*), is abundant in the lower Hudson, but it is primarily a marine fish, which spawns in brackish water and will not be discussed.

SPECIES KEY

1a. Posterior ray in dorsal fin much longer than any of the preceding rays; snout short and blunt, protruding over mouth; origin of dorsal fin posterior to base of pelvic fins . . . .
        Gizzard shad, *Dorosoma cepedianum*

1b. Posterior ray in dorsal fin, not elongated; snout more pointed, lower jaw protruding; dorsal fin directly above or in front of base of pelvic fin 2

2a. A single dark spot on side of body just behind upper end of gill opening; dorsal surface of mandible with a raised crest halfway back (must open mouth to see) (see Figure 8) 3

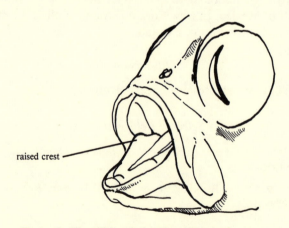

raised crest

Figure 8. Mandible of alewife with raised crest

2b A row of 3 or more dark spots running posteriorly along side of body from upper end of gill opening; dorsal surface of mandible without raised crest halfway back . . . . American shad, *Alosa sapidissima*

3a. Eye diameter less than or equal to snout length; 44–50 gill rakers; in fresh specimens the back is blue, peritoneum black . . . . . Blueback herring, *Alosa aestivalis*

3b. Eye diameter greater than snout length; 39–41 gill rakers; in fresh specimens the back is grayish green; peritoneum silvery . . Alewife, *Alosa pseudoharengus*

Gizzard Shad   *Dorosoma cepedianum* (LeSueur)

Identification

All of the members of the herring family (Clupeidae) are characterized by a series of specialized scales, called scutes, which form a sawtooth edge down the midline of the belly. You can readily appreciate this by running your finger from the front of the anal fin forward toward the throat. The gizzard shad is distinguished from other members of the family by the greatly elongated posterior ray in its dorsal fin. It is blue on the back and silver to white on the sides and belly.

Life History

Gizzard shad spawn between April and June. The female produces 200,000–400,000 adhesive demersal eggs which hatch in 2–4 days. Sexual maturity is reached at 2 years of age. Some individuals have been taken from Lake Erie that were 19 inches long and weighed just a shade under 3 pounds. Most fish, however, are about half that size.

Gizzard shad sometimes suffer extensive die-offs after spawning. Large numbers of dead fish have been reported washed up on shore in the spring.

Gizzard shad feed primarily on algae filtered out of the water and bottom muds. They are equipped with a large number of long thin gill rakers for this purpose. This straining mechanism can be seen by lifting the opercular flaps and observing the white gill rakers on the inside edge of the gills. Gizzard shad are one of the few herbivorous species of fish in New York and possess a gizzard-like structure used to grind and break up plant tissue.

Gizzard shad serve as forage for many game fishes.

Distribution

The gizzard shad ranges from New York south to Florida and west to northeastern Mexico and South Dakota. In New York it has been reported from Lakes Erie, Ontario, and Cayuga.

Other Names

Hickory shad, lake shad, mud shad, sawbelly

American Shad   *Alosa sapidissima* (Wilson)

Identification

The American shad can be distinguished by the presence of scutes, a normal dorsal fin without an extended posterior dorsal ray, and a row of three or more dark spots running posteriorly along the side of the body from the upper end of the gill opening. They are dark bluish-green on their back with silvery sides and belly.

Life History

Shad spend most of their adult life in salt water and only enter fresh water to spawn in the period from April to June in New York. They migrate into the Hudson or Delaware Rivers when the water reaches 50–55°F, and they travel far inland. Spawning occurs at sunset, usually in shallow water near the mouth of tributary creeks. Males and females pair up, swim toward shore, and deposit eggs and sperm as they go. Each female carries an average of 25,000 eggs. The eggs sink to the bottom and are left to fare for themselves. The young shad remain in the stream through the summer, migrating to sea during their first fall. After two to five years in the ocean, where they feed on plankton and grow as large as 30 inches and 12 pounds (the average is much less, more like 2–3 pounds and 19–21 inches long) they return to the same stream to spawn. Shad do not die after spawning and in some cases are known to return in later years to spawn again. Shad which were 11 years old have been found in the Hudson River. Shad also develop landlocked populations which do not return to the sea after hatching but simply grow and reach maturity entirely in fresh water.

Shad provide an excellent sport fishing experience and can be taken readily during their spawning run. They respond nicely to a "shad fly" at dusk and many are also taken with spinning gear and a lead jig. Once a shad is hooked he puts up a most satisfying fight. Care must be taken, however, since the mouth is extremely tender.

The major problems to the management of the shad fishery are the blocking of the spawning rivers by dams and other obstructions, overfishing and high egg and larval mortality. If the adults are unable to reach the spawning grounds, or if the young suffer very high mortality during their seaward migration, the fishery suffers as a consequence.

One of the country's major commercial shad fisheries is in the Hudson River, where up to 100,000 pounds of shad are taken each year.

Distribution

Shad are found all along the Atlantic coast from Newfoundland to Florida. They have been introduced into the Pacific Ocean and now range from California to Alaska. In New York they are caught in the Hudson and Delaware Rivers, and on Long Island. They have also been reported from Lake Ontario.

Other Names

Shad, common shad, Atlantic shad, Delaware River shad

Alewife   *Alosa pseudoharengus* (Wilson)

Identification

Alewives resemble shad and are often confused with them; however, they are easily distinguished by the single dark spot on the side of their bodies behind the gill opening. Shad have a row of three or more spots in this area. Alewivese are dark grey to green on their backs and abruptly shade to silver on their sides and belly, and their mandibles have a raised crest halfway back (Figure 8).

Life History

Alewives are anadromous like the shad and leave the ocean to spawn in fresh water in the spring. They usually spawn in very shallow water. Each female produces between 60,000 and 100,000 eggs. After the young hatch they migrate to the sea, and they return when they are about 3 years old to spawn and complete the cycle.

New York has a number of landlocked populations in some of the Finger Lakes, Lakes Ontario and Erie, and a few Adirondack lakes. These fish are smaller than their counterparts that grow up in the ocean, reaching only 4–5 inches as opposed to 11–12 inches for the sea-run fish. The landlocked alewife spawns from May to August with each female producing 10,000–20,000 eggs. Spawning occurs at night in water 6–12 inches deep over sand or gravel bottoms. Eggs hatch in 2–6 days, and the larvae are pelagic. Adult fish live in open water, usually well below the surface.

Alewives feed primarily on plankton throughout their lives. In lakes where alewives are abundant they can strongly influence the character of the zooplankton population by reducing the numbers of large species of zooplankton in favor of the smaller species. Landlocked alewives may reach 6 inches and 0.1 pound. Some fish from Lake Ontario were found to be 8 years old.

Alewives, although not taken on hook and line, contribute significantly to the sport fishery by providing forage for game fish. In the Finger Lakes, lake trout feed heavily on alewives. The Pacific salmon, introduced into Lake Ontario, utilize alewives as forage. Experiments have been conducted using alewives in Adirondack lakes as forage for brook and lake trout.

Alewife populations may increase more rapidly than those of certain native species such as cisco and whitefish, reducing their populations or, in some cases, eliminating them from the lake altogether. In addition, during the summer alewives are subject to massive die-offs. They wash up on the beach, causing an unpleasant smell and generally creating a nuisance.

Distribution

The marine form of the alewife is found along the Atlantic coast from Newfoundland to North Carolina. It has been introduced to many lakes throughout the U.S. and Canada. In New York it is found in both Great Lakes, many of the Finger Lakes, the Oswego, Genesee, St. Lawrence, Susquehanna, Hudson, and Mohawk Rivers as well as streams on Long Island.

Other Names

Sawbelly, mooneye, Seth Green shad

Selected Herring References

Bodola, A. 1966. "Life History of the Gizzard Shad, *Dorosoma cepedianum* (LeSueur), in Western Lake Erie." *U.S. Fish Wildlife Serv. Fish. Bull.* 65(2): 391–425.

Cheek, R. P. 1968. "The American Shad." *U.S. Fish Wildlife Serv. Fish. Leafl.* 614.

Galligan, J. P. 1962. "Depth Distribution of Lake Trout and Associated Species in Cayuga Lake, New York." *N.Y. Fish Game J.* 9(1): 44–68.

Hildebrand, S. F. 1963. "Family Clupeidae." *Fishes of the Western North Atlantic. Mem. Sears Found. Mar. Res.* 1(3): 257–454.

Miller, R. R. 1957. "Origin and Dispersal of the Alewife, *Alosa pseudoharengus*, and the Gizzard Shad, *Dorosoma cepedianum*, in the Great Lakes. *Trans. Amer. Fish. Soc.* 86(1956): 97–111.

_____, 1960. "Systematics and Biology of the Gizzard Shad (*Dorosoma cepedianum*) and Related Fishes." *U.S. Fish Wildlife Serv. Fish. Bull. 173, vol. 60: 371–92.*

Odell, T. T. 1934. "The Life History and Ecological Relationships of the Alewife (*Pomolobus pseudoharengus* (Wilson)), in Seneca Lake, New York." *Trans. Amer. Fish. Soc.* 64: 118–24.

Pritchard, A. L. 1929. "The Alewife (*Pomolobus pseudoharengus*) in Lake Ontario. *Univ. Toronto Stud. Publ. Ont. Fish. Res. Lab.* 38: 37–54.

Talbot, G. B. 1954. "Factors Associated with Fluctuations in Abundance of Hudson River Shad." *U.S. Fish and Wildlife Serv. Fish. Bull.* 56(101): 373–413.

Mooneye   Family Hiodontidae

Mooneye superficially resemble herring except that they lack scutes, an adipose eyelid, adipose fin, and they do possess a lateral line.

Two species make up this entire family. Both are found exclusively in freshwater habitats of North America. In New York the mooneye *(Hiodon tergisus)* is the only representative.

Mooneye   *Hiodon tergisus* LeSueur

Identification

The mooneye is often confused with the shad and alewife, but it is easily distinguished from them since it lacks the scutes or a sawtooth edge on the midline of its belly, and its dorsal fin rests, at least in part, directly over the anal fin. Mooneyes also have well-developed teeth on their jaws and tongue. The freshwater herrings have the dorsal fin anterior to the anal fin, have scutes, and lack well-developed teeth. The mooneye is light grey on its back and grades quickly to a silvery white on its sides and belly. The fins are silvery white as well. The upper part of the head is delicately shaded with yellow and green.

Life History

Mooneyes are not commonly seen since they live in the open waters of large lakes and rivers. However, because the mooneye is the only representative of the family in New York and is often confused with the alewife, we shall discuss it briefly.

Little is known about its breeding habits except that it is thought to spawn in streams in the spring; with the females laying 10,000–20,000 eggs during that period. Mooneyes have been collected from Lake Erie which were 8 years old. They may grow up to 14 inches in length and approach a pound in weight. They feed on insect larvae, plankton, and an occasional small fish.

A small sport fishery has developed for mooneyes on Lake Champlain where fish are taken using a fly rod and grasshoppers or flies. They feed at the surface so their rises can be easily seen. Once hooked they put up a very game fight, leaping into the air and making long runs. The flesh is excellent eating as well.

Distribution

The mooneye's range extends from south central Canada through the southern Great Lakes to the St. Lawrence–Champlain drainage and then southward west of the Appalachians to Tennessee. In New York they are found in the Great Lakes and St. Lawrence River, Lake Champlain, and the Oswegatchie River.

Other Names

White shad, toothed herring, freshwater herring, river whitefish

Selected Mooneye References

Johnson, G. H. 1951. "An Investigation of the Mooneye *(Hiodon tergisus)*." *Abstract 5th Tech. Sess. Res. Council, Ontario.* 16 p.

Van Oosten, J. 1961. "Records, Ages, and Growth of the Mooneye, *Hiodon tergisus,* of the Great Lakes." *Trans. Amer. Fish. Soc.* 90(2): 170–74.

Salmon and Trout   Family Salmonidae

This is a large and important family of fishes. They possess cycloid scales, soft rays in all fins, an adipose fin, and a pelvic axillary process. The species found in New York can be divided into two subfamilies: the Coregoninae and Salmoninae. Sixty-eight species are known worldwide.

The Coregoninae or cisco and whitefish group is characterized by having a small mouth with the lower jaw not extending behind the eye. Their scales are relatively large with fewer than 100 in the lateral line. Seven species of coregonids have been reported for the state, four of which are found in deep waters of Lake Ontario. These are the bloater *(Coregonus hoyi),* kiyi *(Coregonus kiyi),* shortnose cisco *(Coregonus reighardi),* and blackfin cisco *(Coregonus nigripinnis).* (The blackfin cisco was recorded from Lake Ontario, but it is now considered extinct in that lake.) These deep-water coregonids are relatively rare.

The remaining three coregonids in New York are the whitefish *(Coregonus clupeaformis),* cisco *(Coregonus artedii),* and round whitefish *(Prosopium cylindraceum).* These three species are more common and will be discussed later.

Three genera of Salmoninae occur in New York: *Salvelinus* (char), *Salmo* (trout), and *Oncorhynchus* (Pacific salmon). All three genera are distinguishable from the coregonids by the larger size of their mouth and the smaller size of their scales.

We shall discuss later the two chars found in New York, the brook trout *(Salvelinus fontinalis),* and the lake trout *(Salvelinus namaycush);* the three trout—brown *(Salmo trutta),* rainbow *(Salmo gairdneri),* and the Atlantic salmon *(Salmo salar);* and three of the five Pacific salmon— the coho *(Oncorhynchus kisutch),* the chinook *(Oncorhynchus tshawytscha),* and the kokanee *(Oncorhynchus nerka).*

A key to the salmonids is included below. The characters used to distinguish the Pacific salmon are largely those developed on the West Coast. It is too early to tell whether these characters will be useful in distinguishing our landlocked populations. In addition, a separate key to young trout and salmon less than 5 inches long is provided.

Species Key*

1a. Mouth small, posterior end of upper jaw (maxillary) extends to just below eye (Figure 9); fewer than 100 scales in lateral line 2

1b. Mouth large, posterior end of upper jaw extends well behind eye (Figure 9); more than 100 scales in lateral line 8

2a. Only one single flap between the nostrils (Figure 10); gill rakers fewer than 20 . . . . . Round whitefish, *Prosopium cylindraceum*

2b. Two flaps between nostrils (Figure 10); gill rakers more than 23 3

3a. In side view the snout is pointed (Figure 11); gill rakers between 34 and 52† 4

3b. In side view the snout is rounded (Figure 11); gill rakers fewer than 32 . . . . Lake whitefish, *Coregonus clupeaformis*

4a. Body deepest anterior to middle 5

4b. Body deepest at middle 6

5a. Thin mandible with a knob at the tip; small fish, 6–8 inches long . . . . Kiyi, *Coregonus kiyi*

5b. Mandible heavier and lacking knob at tip; larger fish, 10–15 inches long . . . . Blackfin cisco, *Coregonus nigripinnis*

6a. Gill rakers 43–52 . . . . Cisco, *Coregonus artedii*

6b. Gill rakers 34–43 7

7a. Small fish, 6–8 inches long; mandible with a knob at the tip . . . . Bloater, *Coregonus hoyi*

7b. Larger fish, 12–15 inches long; mandible lacking a knob at the tip . . . . Shortnose cisco, *Coregonus reighardi*

8a. Anal fin with 12 or fewer developed rays, lining of mouth not dark 9

*Key to specimens greater than 5 inches long. For smaller individuals see following key.

†The species that key out here all belong to the subgenus *Leuchichthys* and are extremely difficult to key. The cisco is the most common and wide ranging of the group. The others are found primarily in the deep waters of Lake Ontario.

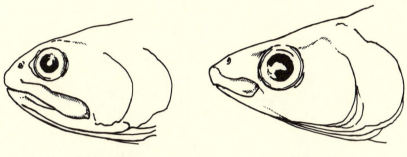

Salmoninae   Coregoninae

Figure 9. Mouths of the two major subdivisions of the family Salmonidae: Salmoninae and Coregoninae

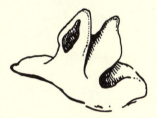

ROUND WHITEFISH   LAKE WHITEFISH

Figure 10. Flaps between the nostrils of round whitefish and lake whitefish

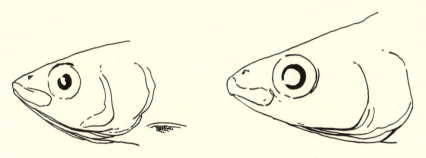

CISCO   LAKE WHITEFISH

Figure 11. Snout of lake whitefish and cisco

8b. Anal fin with 13 or more developed rays; lining of mouth dark, at least in patches 13

9a. Color pattern composed of dark spots on lighter background; lateral line scales less than 175; teeth on shaft of vomer 10

9b. Color pattern composed of light spots on darker background; lateral line scales greater than 175; no teeth on shaft of vomer ... 12

10a. Sides of body with numerous small black spots particularly well developed on caudal fins ..... Rainbow trout, *Salmo gairdneri*

10b. Sides of body with fewer large black spots (many as large or larger than pupil of eye), few if any present on caudal fin 11

11a. Maxillary extends to posterior edge of eye or further in fish longer than 6 inches; many reddish spots well developed on sides and adipose fin (may be faint or absent in populations occupying large lakes); teeth on shaft of vomer well developed (Figure 12)..................... Brown trout, *Salmo trutta*

11b. Maxillary extends to just below posterior edge of pupil, rarely to posterior edge of eye; no reddish spots; teeth on shaft of vomer weak and deciduous ...... Atlantic salmon, *Salmo salar*

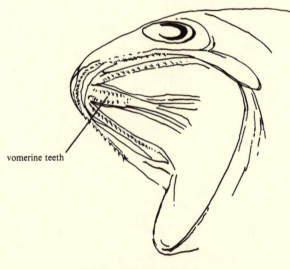

vomerine teeth

Figure 12. Vomerine teeth in brown trout

12a. Lower fins with the leading edge white, followed by a black stripe; body with small red spots encircled in blue; caudal fin with little or no fork; gill rakers 9-12; mandibular pores 7-8 . . . . Brook trout, *Salvelinus fontinalis*

12b. Lower fins without black stripe and white stripe poorly developed; body not brightly colored, generally greyish; caudal fin definitely forked; gill rakers 12-14; mandibular pores 9-10 . . . . Lake trout, *Salvelinus namaycush*

13a. Body without distinct black spots, but some very fine speckling may be present . . . . Kokanee, *Oncorhynchus nerka*

13b. Body with distinct large black spots, the largest approaching the size of the pupil of the eye 14

14a. Fish can be easily picked up by the tail; both lobes of caudal fin with black spots; first rays of anal fin, when depressed, reach less than ⅔ of the way to end of anal fin . . . . . Chinook salmon,
Oncorhynchus tshawytscha

14b. Fish cannot be picked up easily by the tail; no spots on lower lobe of caudal fin; first rays of anal fin when depressed reach more than ⅔ of the way to end of anal fin . . . . . . Coho salmon,
Oncorhynchus kisutch

Key to Young Salmon and Trout 2-5 Inches Long

1a. Principal anal rays 8-12 2

1b. Principal anal rays 13-19 6

2a. Dorsal fin with dark spots and/or black first dorsal ray 3

2b. Dorsal fin lacking dark markings . . . . Lake trout,
Salvelinus namaycush

3a. Red or yellow spots between parr marks generally less than or equal to width of parr marks at lateral line 4

3b. Red or yellow spots missing; space between dark parr marks generally greater than width of parr marks at lateral line . . . . . .
Rainbow trout, *Salmo gairdneri*

4a. Caudal fin deeply forked, shortest rays approximately one half of the length of the longest; pectoral fin as long as depressed dorsal fin . . . . Atlantic salmon, *Salmo salar*

4b. Caudal fin shallowly forked, shortest rays greater than one half the length of the longest; pectoral fin shorter than depressed dorsal 5

5a. Eight or 9 parr marks; sides below lateral line without small dark spots . . . . Brook trout, *Salvelinus fontinalis*

5b. Approximately 11 parr marks; sides below lateral line with small dark spots . . . . Brown trout, *Salmo trutta*

6a. Parr marks short and stubby, none taller than diameter of eye . . . . Kokanee, *Oncorhynchus nerka*

6b. Parr marks tall, the largest greater than diameter of eye 7

7a. Adipose fin with pigmentation heavier on dorsal and posterior edge, less pigment in center; anal fin lacking dark pigment . . . . Chinook salmon, *Oncorhynchus tshawytscha*

7b. Adipose fin evenly pigmented; anal fin with dark pigment posterior to white leading edge . . . . Coho salmon *Oncorhynchus kisutch*

Round Whitefish   *Prosopium cylindraceum* (Pallas)

Identification

Round whitefish are distinguishable by the small mouth and the single flap of tissue between the anterior and posterior opening of each nostril. Lake whitefish and cisco have a double flap of tissue. In addition, the 13–20 gill rakers of the round whitefish are short and stubby, whereas the 23 or more gill rakers in the cisco and whitefish are long and slender. They are generally dark gray dorsally grading through silver to white ventrally. Blue, purple, green, and even a yellow sheen is apparent on the sides of adults at times. Young have several horizontal rows of black spots on their sides.

Life History

Round whitefish spawn in the fall, usually in November, over shallow shoal areas or off the mouth of streams over gravel bottoms.

They pair up and broadcast their eggs over the bottom. A single female may carry 2,000–10,000 eggs. Once spawning has occurred, the eggs are abandoned.

The eggs incubate over the winter and hatch in about 140 days. The young begin feeding on plankton. As they grow their diet switches to bottom invertebrates, with mayfly, caddisfly, and midge larvae as well as small molluscs appearing most commonly in their stomachs.

They may achieve an age of 14 years and a length of 20 inches, but adults are more commonly 4–7 years old and 9–14 inches long.

Round whitefish prefer deep, clear lakes, but generally venture no deeper than 150 feet. They enter shallow water only to spawn.

They can be taken by anglers and their flesh is excellent; however, they are very lightly exploited by fishermen. Lake trout and other large salmonids may depend on them as forage.

Distribution

The round whitefish is widely distributed throughout Canada, Alaska, and northeastern Asia. In New York it is found primarily in the Adirondacks where it is relatively rare. It has also been reported from Lake Ontario.

Other Names

Adirondack frostfish, frostfish, Menominee whitefish

Lake Whitefish *Coregonus clupeaformis* (Mitchill)

Identification

The lake whitefish is distinguishable from the rest of the coregonids by its rounded snout and the double flap between its nostrils. It is usually silvery gray to white with little coloration.

Life History

Lake whitefish spawn from October to December, depending on the temperature and the locality. Males are the first to arrive on the spawning grounds, which are near shore in shallow water, less than 20 feet deep, over a gravelly or sandy bottom. Spawning occurs primarily at night with females rising to the surface, discharging eggs as they go. Males follow, fertilizing the eggs. The eggs are only slightly heavier than water and sink gently to the bottom. Females carry about 10,000 eggs for each pound of body weight, thus producing 10,000–75,000 eggs per fish. Spawning lasts for about 10 days, with many repetitions of the spawning act.

The eggs hatch in 120 to 140 days and the fry begin feeding within two weeks on microscopic crustaceans. At this time the young whitefish are usually found in water less than two feet deep. As they grow they move into deeper water until finally as adults they are found in water 60 feet or deeper. When they reach an inch in length their mouth turns downward, and they begin feeding off the bottom on crustaceans, molluscs, and insects.

Whitefish up to 20 pounds have been reported, but the average is less than 4 pounds. They grow slowly and many take up to 16 years to reach such a size.

Whitefish comprise a desirable portion of the commercial catch in Lake Ontario. They are light and delicately flavored, providing a high-quality food.

Angling for whitefish is not as well developed as it could be. In Otsego Lake there is a fishery for whitefish called Otsego bass. Whitefish can be taken on flies when in shallow water; or by jigging, or using small pieces of fish on a small hook when they are in deep water. The mouth of the whitefish is delicate and great care must be taken in setting the hook and retrieving the fish so that the hook does not tear out of the mouth.

Distribution

The whitefish are distributed throughout Canada and Alaska and extend into many lakes in the northern tier of the states. In New York they have been found in the following lakes: Otsego, Caroga, Canada, Champlain, Saranac, Placid, Clear, Ontario, Erie, Raquette, and the Finger Lakes. They undoubtedly exist in many other deep cool lakes as well.

Other Names

Common whitefish, shad

Cisco   *Coregonus artedii* LeSueur

Identification

The cisco most resembles the lake whitefish, but can be distinguished from it by the shape of the snout. In the cisco it is more pointed and the mouth is terminal (Figure 11). The back is green to blue, the sides silvery with an iridescent sheen, while the belly and fins are generally white.

Life History

Although ciscoes move into shallow water early in the fall, spawning takes place many weeks later, usually late in November or early December. Spawning appears to be a group activity which involves many individuals. The eggs are broadcast on the bottom and receive no parental care. They hatch in 110–130 days. The fry begin life feeding on plankton and most will continue to feed on plankton all their lives. Occasionally, mayflies or small minnows are consumed. Ciscoes may live up to 10 years and achieve a size approaching 20 inches; most are smaller, however.

Ciscoes are cold water fish preferring water cooler than 60° F. Consequently, during the summer they are generally found in deep water, moving into shallow areas only when the temperature has dropped.

Ciscoes, like lake whitefish, are a part of the commercial fishery in the Great Lakes. They are a delightful food fish and consequently in great demand. Surprisingly, relatively few sportsmen fish for them. They will take a fly when a large hatch is occurring in the spring, and they can be taken through the ice, fishing fairly deeply with jigs.

Distribution

The range of the cisco is from Quebec west to Alberta and north to the Northwest Territories. Its range dips into the United States in the Great Lakes and upper Mississippi drainages. In New York it has been found in the following lakes: Erie, Ontario, Champlain, George, Oneida, Tupper Otsego, Chautauqua, Hedges, and many of the Finger Lakes.

Other Names

Lake herring, tullibee

Brook Trout   *Salvelinus fontinalis* (Mitchill)

Identification

The brook trout, as with all salmonids, is characterized by the presence of an adipose fin and a pelvic axillary process, and by the absence of barbels around the mouth. Brook trout in New York are distinguished from other trout in that the color pattern on their bodies is basically a scattering of light spots on a darker background. The light spots on the dorsal part of the body are commonly worm-like and irregular in shape. Toward the ventral part of the body the spots become circular. Scattered among the light spots on the side are a few bright red spots surrounded by a blue ring. The pelvic and anal fins are orange to pink with conspicuous white leading edges followed by a dark stripe.

Life History

Spawning occurs in the fall between September and December. In most cases mature adults move into headwater streams, selecting a site with a good gravel bottom and substantial flow of cold, clear water. A depression in the gravelly bottom is dug by the female while the male stands guard, chasing other fish away. The female faces upstream, and while lying on her side, vibrates her body, violently kicking out gravel, which is carried a short distance downstream. This process is continued until a nest several inches deep is created. She will frequently lie on the nest, extending her anal fin as if to measure the correct depth during the digging phase. Eventually, she is satisfied and the male moves onto the nest with her. She places her vent as close as possible to the deepest part of the nest and extrudes anywhere from a few hundred to several thousand eggs. At the same time the male produces a cloud of sperm that fertilize the eggs. Immediately after spawning the female moves upstream and begins to cover the nest by sweeping her tail across the bottom, dislodging gravel which falls into the nest and covers the eggs. The male stands guard for a few minutes after spawning but quickly loses interest and abandons his post. Females carry up to 7,000 eggs and thus may spawn more than once. In fact, it has been observed that after spawning a female will frequently move a short distance upstream and begin constructing a new nest.

The eggs develop slowly during the fall and winter. They may take as long as 142 days if the water is cold (35°F) or as short as 28 days if the water is warm (59°F). Normally in New York streams the water temperature is near freezing in the winter and thus the incubation period lasts most of the winter. After hatching the young fish remain in the redd, receiving nourishment from their large yolk sac. They begin feeding about a month later and abandon the nest.

Brook trout are not long-lived, usually surviving only until their fourth or fifth year, although some strains in Canada are known to live for 10 years.

Young trout begin feeding on microcrustaceans and small insects. As they grow they continue to feed on insects and other stream invertebrates.

Large trout may switch to feeding on fish, amphibians, or even small mammals. Most brook trout in New York are less than 14 inches long. It is possible, however, for them to exceed 14 pounds and 31 inches in unusually productive water as is evidenced by the capture of one fish this large in Canada. Work is now under way to determine if some of the fast-growing Canadian strains might be suitable for introduction into New York waters. If so, fishing for trophy size brook trout may be possible in New York. The record brook trout for New York is 8 pounds, 8 ounces, and was taken in 1908 from Punchbowl Pond in Sullivan County.

Brook trout are one of the most sensitive game fish in New York. They are very intolerant of environmental degradation. They need water whose temperature rarely exceeds 79° F and then for only short periods. They do better when the water remains below 65° F. In addition, oxygen levels must be above 5–6 ppm, the bottom must not be silted over, and good sand or gravel should be present for spawning. Consequently, as land was cleared in lowland areas, farms were worked, homes built, and industries started, the water suitable for brook trout diminished. The trout survived only in headwater streams and ponds where the environmental conditions remained suitable. Unfortunately, headwater streams are small and thus give rise to small fish.

To support an important sport fishery, brook trout are stocked by the New York State Department of Environmental Conservation in waters throughout the state. These fish are reared in hatcheries and have had a long history of domestication. Cornell fishery biologists have shown that domestic strains have a lower survival rate than wild strains. This could be due to the fact that the wild strain has greater stamina than the domestic strain. In contrast, the domestic strain grows more rapidly in the hatchery, producing larger fish for stocking.

Brook trout are one of the fish most sought after by the angler. They readily take flies or other artificial lures, provide a showy fight, and are delicious in the pan. In addition, they are one of our prettiest fish and are commonly taken in beautiful surroundings. In recognition of this the brook trout has been designated the official New York State fish.

Brook trout can be taken on dry flies, wet flies, or nymphs in a variety of patterns. Check with local fishermen as to successful types. Larger trout are commonly taken on spoons or spinners. They may also be taken on live bait.

Distribution

The brook trout's original range ran from Georgia north to Labrador and the Hudson Bay region and thence south to the Great Lakes region. It has been introduced in other parts of the world as well, but due to its sensitivity it is not as widespread as the brown or rainbow trout. In New York it can be found in every major watershed where habitat is suitable.

Other Names

Speckled trout, native trout, square-tailed trout, eastern brook trout, speckled char

Lake Trout   *Salvelinus namaycush* (Walbaum)

Identification

The lake trout, like the brook trout, is a char and thus characterized by light spots on a dark background. The black stripe on the lower fin is missing and the white stripe on the leading edge of the lower fins is not well developed. The lake trout is not a brightly colored fish and its caudal fin is forked. Each of the above characteristics will distinguish the lake trout from brook trout.

Life History

Lake trout spawn in the fall between October and December. They spawn in lakes, generally in water less than 100 feet deep. They deposit their heavy non-adhesive eggs over the bottom in naturally occurring cavities. Females carry 700–800 eggs per pound body weight, so a 10-pound female may carry 7,000–8,000 eggs.

Eggs hatch in about 110 days and the young begin feeding on zooplankton and small insect larvae. They soon begin to feed on a wide array of insects and crustaceans, with one of the favorites being the possum shrimp (*Mysis relicta*). Larger lake trout utilize fish for forage such as alewives, shiners, suckers, sculpins, sticklebacks, troutperch, whitefish, and smelt.

Lake trout have been reported that weighed more than 100 pounds. This is very rare. It is quite rare even to see a fish in excess of 30 or 40 pounds. Much more common are fish in the 2–10 pound category. The record catch in New York was a 31-pound fish caught in Follensby Pond in 1922.

During the warmer part of the year lake trout are found in the deep cool water of large lakes. They generally prefer water with adequate oxygen that stays between 44–55°F. In late fall, winter, and early spring they may forage in shallow water as long as the temperature stays below 50° F. In New York the lake trout is at the southern extremity of its range. It is a northern species that hasn't adapted well to our southern lakes. Because of the warming of the surface waters of our lakes in summer the lake trout is forced to seek deeper cooler waters. If the lake is shallow, or if, due to eutrophication, the deeper waters do not contain oxygen, the lake trout will not survive the summer. Consequently, lake trout are found only in large lakes which still maintain adequate oxygen in their deeper waters.

The lake trout was formerly a very important part of the commercial catch of fishermen in the Great Lakes. Its numbers declined due to a variety of causes and now it is too rare to contribute significantly to the catch.

It is also highly prized by the sport fishermen. In the spring and fall it can be taken on light spinning gear or even on flies in shallow water. When taken in this manner it demonstrates its fighting qualities. More commonly, however, it is taken during the summer by trolling at great depths with wire line and a spinning rig. Lake trout are fine eating fish, although some tend to be a little oily.

Distribution

Lake trout are generally distributed throughout Canada and Alaska. They also extend into the continental United States in New England, New York, Pennsylvania, Michigan, Wisconsin, Minnesota, Montana, and Idaho. In New York they are known from the following lakes: Blue Mountain, Raquette, Eaton, Sagamore, Wolf, West Canada, Green, Upper Saranac, George, Placid, Chazy, Millsite, Star, the Fulton Chain, the Finger Lakes, Ontario, Erie, Champlain, and possibly other deep Adirondack lakes.

Other Names

Laker, togue, mackinaw

Brown Trout   *Salmo trutta* Linneaus

Identification

Brown trout, as with other trout and salmon, are characterized by dark spots on a lighter background. In the case of brown trout these spots are large (many approximately the size of the pupil of the eye) and rarely present on the caudal fin. They are cast against the light brown background of the body. The belly is creamy white. In addition, numerous red or orange spots are present on the sides. The brown trout has 9–10 anal rays. Brown trout can often be confused with landlocked salmon; however, if you look at the maxillary you will see that it extends at least to the posterior edge of the eye in the brown trout, whereas in the salmon the maxillary only reaches the rear edge of the pupil.

Life History

Spawning occurs in the fall, usually in October or November, in streams with good gravel bottoms. Spawning behavior is similar to the brook trout. A female may carry anywhere from 200–2,000 eggs. Young hatch in 100–165 days, depending on temperature. They begin feeding on very small bottom organisms such as young black fly, mayfly, and stonefly larvae. They continue to feed on bottom insects as they grow, moving to progressively larger individuals as they are capable of handling them. In addition, their menus expand to include amphipods, molluscs, terrestrial insects washed into the stream, and fish.

Brown trout may live up to 9 or 10 years, achieving a size of 20 pounds or better. Fish up to 40 pounds have been reported, but the usual fish caught is less than 1 pound. The record for New York weighed 22 pounds, 4 ounces, and came from Keuka Lake.

Brown trout are found in both streams and lakes, but spawning almost always occurs in streams. The young remain in the stream for several years, migrating back to the lake where they mature and return to spawn some years later. Stream populations, of course, spend their entire life in the stream. Brown trout are more tolerant of difficult environmental conditions than brook trout and consequently have replaced them in many marginal habitats.

Brown trout are highly regarded as a sport fish. Izaak Walton wrote many lines about the joys of fishing for them. Since that time brown trout have continued to give millions of anglers hours of enjoyable fishing. It is one of the more difficult fish to catch. It is wary and suspicious and consequently more of a challenge than brook or rainbow trout. Brown trout can be taken on flies, spinners, or live bait such as worms, grasshoppers, hellagramites, or minnows.

Distribution

Originally brown trout were found only in Europe and western Asia, but they have been widely introduced throughout the world. The first brown trout to arrive in the United States were stocked in New York in

1883. They have since been introduced in most of the suitable waters of the state. No major drainage in New York is without brown trout.

Other Names

German brown trout, Lochleven trout, brown, brownie

Landlocked Salmon   *Salmo salar* Linnaeus

Identification

Landlocked salmon are simply populations of Atlantic salmon that have become isolated from the ocean and thus spend their entire lives in fresh water. They bear a resemblance to brown trout, but the brown trout has two rows of strong teeth on the vomer while the landlocked salmon has a single row of weak deciduous teeth. In addition, the maxillary extends no further than the back of the eye in Atlantic salmon; whereas, in brown trout the maxillary extends well behind the eye. The back and sides are grayish-brown with large dark spots, grading to olive and eventually grayish white on the belly.

Life History

Landlocked salmon move to the mouth of spawning streams in September. They do not spawn, however, until October or November after migrating some distance up stream. The female digs a redd in the gravel to receive her eggs. She is attended by several males who are continually bickering about who is her rightful mate. After the nest is constructed, and usually at night, she deposits her eggs in the nest, which are immediately fertilized by one of the accompanying males. This process is repeated in new mating sites until the female is spent. A female may carry up to 4,000 eggs. Eggs hatch in approximately 100 days. The young spend several years in the stream before returning to the lake. Growth accelerates when they get to the lake and can begin feeding on forage fish. Prior to that their diet in the stream is predominantly insects.

The oldest fish reported was a 13-year-old specimen taken in Scotland; however, most fish do not reach their 10th birthday. Average size is between 16 and 28 inches. The New York record weighed 18 pounds, 8 ounces, and was taken from the Oswego River in 1978. Sexual maturity is reached between three and five years of age. Unlike Pacific salmon the landlocked salmon does not always die after spawning and can return to spawn again.

The landlocked salmon without a doubt is one of the finest sport fish in the state. It can be taken on a fly, spinner or live bait, and the fight is spectacular with many long runs and jumps. Efforts are being made by the New York State Department of Environmental Conservation to establish this species in a number of the large deep lakes of New York State.

Distribution

The Atlantic salmon (as distinguished from the landlocked salmon) is widely distributed throughout the north Atlantic from Portugal northward and westward to Canada and originally as far south as the Connecticut River. The landlocked salmon in New York is found in Lake George, Lake Champlain, Indian Lake, Schroon Lake, Cayuga Lake, and Lake Ontario.

Other Names

Atlantic salmon, sebago salmon

Rainbow Trout   *Salmo gairdneri* Richardson

Identification

The rainbow is a trout with many small dark spots on a lighter background. The spots are particularly well developed on the caudal fin. Brown trout and landlocked salmon have larger spots, with few on the caudal fin. Rainbow trout have 12 or fewer anal rays. Pacific salmon (coho, chinook, and kokanee) have 13 or more anal rays. Rainbow trout are quite variable in their coloration. Fish living in lakes will be light and silvery colored, often referred to as "steelheads," while stream-dwelling rainbows will be much darker and more heavily spotted. The back is dark blue to brown, grading to silver on its belly, and its side contains a characteristic pink to red band.

Life History

The rainbow, unlike other New York salmonids, spawns in the spring, in streams over good gravel. In the Finger Lakes and possibly other areas as well, some rainbows migrate into the tributary streams in the fall, but wait until the spring to spawn, while others migrate into the stream in March or April.

Redd construction and spawning itself is very similar to the brook trout. A female may carry 2,000–3,000 eggs. Due to warmer water temperatures, the incubation period is shorter for rainbows than it is for fall spawners, with most young hatching within 60 days.

Stream-dwelling rainbows feed on bottom invertebrates and terrestrial insects washed into the stream. Lake-dwelling rainbows also feed on insects, but cladocerans and small fish make up a substantial portion of their diet as well. Rainbows prefer water cooler than 70° F, but they can survive temperatures up to 80° F for short periods of time. It is probably the trout in New York most tolerant of warm water and thus along with the brown trout most likely to survive in marginal habitat.

Rainbow trout live for 6 or 7 years. Lake rainbows may reach 20–22 inches and 3 or 4 pounds during that time. Stream rainbows are usually smaller, 10–12 inches and less than a pound. The New York record is 21 pounds, 9 ounces and was taken in the Salmon River.

An opportunity to catch lake rainbows in streams occurs every spring in the major tributaries of the Finger Lakes, such as Cayuga Inlet, Catherine Creek, and Grout Brook. Excellent runs also occur in the Salmon River and its tributaries. Numerous large rainbows leaving the lake and migrating upstream to spawn are concentrated in a relatively small area and thus offer some excellent sport. In addition, before the fishing season opens, you can spend an enjoyable day walking the stream, observing trout digging redds or leaping obstacles in the stream.

Rainbow trout are excellent game fish and can be taken in a wide variety of ways, using flies, spinners, spoons, live bait, cheese, and even marshmallows.

Distribution

The original range of the rainbow was in lakes and streams of the Rocky Mountains and coastal areas from northern Mexico to Alaska. It has since been introduced all over the world. One of the earliest was an introduction in New York in 1874. It is now found in all of the major drainages of the state where suitable habitat is present.

Other Names

Steelhead, steelhead trout, steelhead rainbow, Kamloop trout

Coho Salmon   *Oncorhynchus kisutch* (Walbaum)

Identification

All Pacific salmon in New York in the genus *Oncorhynchus* (coho, chinook, and kokanee) can be distinguished from other trout and salmon by the fact that they have at least 13 soft rays in their anal fin. Trout and Atlantic salmon have 12 or fewer soft anal rays. Coho have conspicuous black spots on their back and the upper lobe of their caudal fin. Chinook have similar black spots, but they extend onto the lower lobe as well. Kokanee have no conspicuous black spots, but some speckling from minute spots may occur. The coho is dark blue to green on its back and grades through bright silver on its side and eventually to white on the belly.

Life History

In New York coho move into spawning streams tributary to Lake Ontario and Erie, during September and early October. Some natural spawning occurs at least in tributaries to the Salmon River, but whether it is adequate to maintain the population without stocking is unknown. The general outline of coho spawning and reproduction is as follows. The female chooses the spawning site, generally preferring a location with small to medium sized gravel at the head of a riffle, right where the smooth water of the upstream pool begins to roughen as it flows over the riffle. The female digs the nest by violent undulations of her body while lying on her side close to the bottom. Males never assist in this process. Frequently more than one male accompanies each female, but only one male is dominant and the others are considered accessory males. After the nest is constructed the dominant male joins the female in the nest and spawning occurs. If other males are present they usually take advantage of this opportunity and dart into the nest and release sperm. A female may spawn more than once. She carries 1,400–6,000 eggs. Not long after spawning is finished, the adult fish dies. The eggs hatch in 35–50 days in natural spawning streams of the west coast. Hatching, if spawning is successful, is probably delayed in New York streams because of the cold winters. The young remain in the stream for a year, feeding heavily on aquatic insects, and then they migrate downstream to the lake. Although they remain in the lake for only two summer growing seasons, growth is quite rapid and they may reach 24 inches and 8 pounds before they begin the spawning run which leads to their eventual death. The New York record is 18 pounds, 7 ounces, taken from Lake Ontario in 1979. In the lake they are highly piscivorous, feeding in Lake Ontario primarily on alewives.

Coho are not native to New York. They are found in streams along the west coast of North America from northern California to Alaska and over to Russia and Japan. They normally migrate to the ocean after their first stream year. In 1968 they were introduced in New York in Lake Ontario and Lake Erie in the hopes that they would take hold and provide a fishery similar to the highly successful one developed in Michigan. It is now clear, based on the successful establishment of this species, that coho can do well in New York's Great Lakes.

The best fishing for coho occurs as they congregate off the mouth of spawning streams. Trolling with spinners or spoons, spin casting, or even fly fishing with streamers are all good methods at this time. After they enter the stream to spawn they stop feeding and are much more difficult to catch. Snagging with multiple hooks is then allowed. The coho is beginning to appear in the catch of commercial fishermen both here and in Canada.

Distribution

In New York the coho has been introduced in Lake Ontario and Lake Erie and may be found in the Niagara River.

Other Names

Coho, silver salmon

Chinook Salmon   *Oncorhynchus tshawytscha* (Walbaum)

Identification

Chinook, with large black spots on both the upper and lower lobe of their caudal fin and 14–16 anal rays, are readily distinguishable from other salmonids. They are blue or bluish-green on their backs, grading to silver on their sides and white on the belly.

Life History

Chinook are the largest of the Pacific salmon and in 1969 were stocked in Lake Ontario. This is the third attempt to get a population started in Lake Ontario since the first try in 1874.

Chinook are fall spawners, moving into streams in September or October. Spawning behavior is similar to that of the coho. Each female may carry 2,000–14,000 eggs depending on her size. Young hatch the following spring. The fry remain in the stream for several months before descending to the lake. They feed almost exclusively on aquatic insects at this time, in contrast to the coho, which will take fish in the stream if available. In the lake they spend two to three years feeding on forage fish such as alewives, smelt or shad, and grow quite rapidly. Freshwater populations in large reservoirs in California had individuals reaching 15–18 pounds in three years. In Alaska a sea run chinook weighing 126 pounds has been reported. Lake Ontario fish are smaller than sea run fish, but some in the 13–20-pound class have been taken. The largest fish taken to date in New York was a 44 pound, 12 ounce, individual taken from the Salmon River in 1979.

Angling for chinook is done off the mouths of spawning streams, usually by trolling or by snagging in the stream proper. A minnow attached so as to have a wobbling action when trolled is usually quite successful. It is too early to tell how much chinook will contribute to the commercial fishery. If they become well established they may become a significant factor in the commercial catch.

Distribution

The chinook ranges throughout the north Pacific from southern California to Alaska over to Russia and south to Japan. In New York, it can be found in Lake Ontario, Lake Erie, and the Niagara River.

Other Names

King salmon, tyee

Kokanee   *Oncorhynchus nerka* (Walbaum)

Identification

Kokanee are a landlocked form of sockeye salmon. They have 13–14 anal rays and no distinct black spots on their body or fins which separates them from coho and chinook salmon. Their coloration ranges from dark blue on the back through silver on the sides to white on the belly.

Life History

They spawn from September to December in streams tributary to the lake or even in shallow areas along the lake shore. The female digs a nest; spawning occurs; and in a few weeks or months the spawning fish die. Females normally carry about 450 eggs. The young hatch in 48–140 days, depending on water temperature. After leaving the nest the young spend very little time in the stream, but move directly to the lake. They feed on plankton throughout most of their lives, occasionally eating insects when these are abundant. They mature at age four, for the most part, and range in size when mature from 8–12 inches. They prefer water between 50–59° F and thus are normally found in deep water during the summer.

Kokanee can be taken on hook and line even though they are primarily plankton feeders. Trolling, still-fishing, or fly fishing are the most widely used techniques. When trolling follow a spinner with a small hook baited with a worm or maggot. Bait for still fishing should be either a worm, maggot, or, better yet, a piece of corn. When kokanee are feeding on insects at the surface they can be taken on flies too. They are very tasty but have a high oil content and will spoil if not properly handled.

Distribution

Kokanee are found in coastal lakes around the North Pacific Ocean from California to Alaska, Russia, and south to Japan. They have also been introduced in Lake Colby, Little Green Pond, Long Pond, Pine Pond, and Clear Pond in the Champlain drainage; Twin Lake, Bug Lake, and Mitchell Ponds in the Oswegatchie and Black drainages; and Glass Lake in the Hudson drainage.

Other Names

Sockeye, landlocked sockeye, red salmon

Selected Trout and Salmon References

Behnke, R. J. 1972. "The Systematics of Salmonid Fishes of Recently Glaciated Lakes." *J. Fish. Res. Bd. Canada* 29: 639–71.

Bridges, C. H., and J. W. Mullan. 1958. "A Compendium of the Life History and Ecology of the Eastern Brook Trout, *Salvelinus fontinalis* (Mitchill)." *Mass. Fish. Bull.* 23: 38 p.

Clemens, W. A. 1928. "The Food of Trout from the Streams of Oneida County, New York State." *Trans. Amer. Fish. Soc.* 58: 181–95.

Daly, R., V. A. Hacker, and L. Wiegert. 1962. "The Lake Trout, Its Life History, Ecology, and Management." *Wis. Cons. Dept. Publ.* 233: 15 p.

Dymond, J. R. 1963. "Family Salmonidae." In *Fishes of the Western North Atlantic. Mem. Sears Found. Mar. Res.* 1(3): 457–502.

Frost, W. E., and M. E. Brown. 1967. *The Trout.* London: Collins, 268 p.

Haig-Brown, R. L. 1967. "Canada's Pacific Salmon." *Dept. Fish. Can.* 29 p.

Hartman, W. L. 1959. "Biology and Vital Statistics of Rainbow Trout in the Finger Lakes Region, New York." *N. Y. Fish Game J.* 6(2): 121–78.

Hatch, R. W. 1957. "Success of Natural Spawning of Rainbow Trout in the Finger Lakes Region of New York." *N. Y. Fish Game J.* 4(1): 69–87.

Havey, K. A., and K. Warner. 1970. "The Landlocked Salmon *(Salmo salar).* Its Life History and Management in Maine." *Sport Fish. Inst. Washington, and Maine Dept. Inland Fish. Game.* 129 p.

Heacox, C. E. 1974. *The Complete Brown Trout.* New York: Winchester Press.

Hile, R. 1936. "Age and Growth of the Cisco, *Leucichthys artedi* (Le-Sueur), in the Lakes of the Northeastern Highlands, Wisconsin." *Bull. U.S. Bur. Fish.* 48(19): 211–317.

Johnson, J. H. 1978. "Natural Reproduction and Juvenile Ecology of Pacific Salmon and Steelhead Trout in Tributaries of the Salmon River, New York." M.S. thesis, SUNY College of Environmental Science and Forestry. 133 p.

Normandeau, D. A. 1969. "Life History and Ecology of the Round Whitefish *Prosopium cylindraceum* (Pallas), of Newfound Lake, Bristol, New Hampshire." *Trans. Amer. Fish. Soc.* 98(1): 7–13.

Northcote, T. G., ed. 1969. "Symposium on Salmon and Trout in Streams." H. R. MacMillan lectures in fisheries. Univ. British Columbia, Vancouver, B.C. 388 p.

Van Oosten, J., and H. J. Deason. 1939. "The Age, Growth, and Feeding Habits of the Whitefish, *Coregonus clupeafornis* (Mitchill), of Lake Champlain." *Trans. Amer. Fish. Soc.* 68: 152–62.

Smelt   Family Osmeridae

Smelt are found in fresh water and marine environments. They are small fish with large mouths, an adipose fin, cycloid scales, and a lateral line. They have no pelvic axillary process.

The smelt family is composed of 10 species. Only one occurs in New York.

Rainbow Smelt   *Osmerus mordax* (Mitchill)

Identification

Smelt are minnow-like fish which can be distinguished from all other fishes in the state by the presence of an adipose fin and a lack of either barbels, pelvic axillary process, or spines in the dorsal fin. They are light green on the back with silvery sides or belly. Their color tends to darken in stained waters such as occur in Adirondack lakes.

Life History

Smelt are primarily marine fish that enter fresh water to spawn. However, many have become landlocked and thus move from a lake to a tributary stream to spawn. This usually occurs around the time of ice break-up. Adults swim into the stream at night, rarely progressing more than a few hundred yards upstream. The female chooses a position over gravel or sand and three or four smaller males position themselves downstream. She then produces up to 50,000 eggs which are fertilized by the waiting males. The eggs attach to the bottom and the young, after hatching, return to the lake and begin feeding on plankton. Growth in females is more rapid than males. A large female may be 10 inches long and weigh ¼ pound. A large male, in contrast, would be only 8½ inches long and weigh ⅙ pound. Smelt are lake-dwelling fish, preferring cool water. They feed on plankton, often migrating inshore at night in search of food.

Smelt are an excellent food fish and are sought by both commercial fishermen as well as sport fishermen. The customary procedure is for anglers to gather at night in groups, build a bonfire, and line up along the banks of a spawning stream. As the smelt swim upstream they are captured with a dip net.

Distribution

Originally, smelt ranged along the Atlantic coast from New Jersey to Labrador. Landlocked populations occurred throughout New England and the Maritime Provinces of Canada. The original range of the smelt has been greatly extended by introductions. In New York smelt are found in the following lakes or reservoirs: Raquette, Indian, Neversink, Ontario, Schroon, Champlain, Canadarago, Fulton Chain, and the Finger Lakes, as well as streams on Long Island.

Other Name

Smelt

Selected Smelt References

Bigelow, H. B., and W. C. Schroeder. 1963. "Family Osmeridae." *Fishes of the Western North Atlantic. Mem. Sears Mar. Res.* 1(3): 533–97.

Zilliox, R. G., and W. D. Youngs. 1958. "Further Studies on the Smelt of Lake Champlain." *N. Y. Fish and Game J.* 5(2): 164–74.

Pike   Family Esocidae

Pike are elongate physostomous fishes with the dorsal and anal fin located far back near the forked caudal fin. The head and particularly the snout is somewhat flattened. The jaws are well armed with teeth.

The family is composed of 5 species, of which 4 are found in New York.

SPECIES KEY

1a. Prominent dark vertical bar extends downward from eye; operculum and cheeks completely scaled (Figure 13); dorsal and caudal fins without dark markings 2

1b. Dark vertical bar under eye absent or faint; lower half of operculum without scales (Figure 13) dorsal and caudal fins with dark markings 3

2a. Dark vertical or oblique bars on sides of body; snout shorter, distance from snout tip to center of pupil less than distance from center of pupil to posterior edge of operculum; branchiostegal rays usually 11–13 . . . . . . Grass pickerel, *Esox americanus*

2b. Dark chain-like pattern on sides of body; snout longer, distance from snout tip to center of pupil greater than distance from

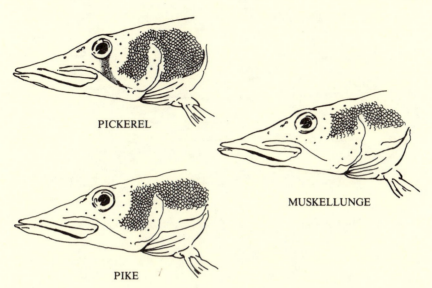

Figure 13. Scale pattern on cheek and opercle

center of pupil to posterior edge of operculum, branchiostegal
rays usually 14–16 . . . . Chain pickerel, *Esox niger*

3a. Cheek completely scaled (Figure 13); light spots on body and
vertical fins; mandibular pores 5 or fewer (Figure 14); branchiostegal rays 14–16 . . . . Northern pike, *Esox lucius*

3b. Cheek without scales on lower half; dark spots on body and vertical fins; mandibular pores 6–9; branchiostegal rays 17–19 . . . .
Muskellunge, *Esox masquinongy*

Grass Pickerel or Redfin Pickerel   *Esox americanus*

Identification

The two species of pickerel are easily distinguished from pike and
muskellunge in that both their cheek and operculum are completely
scaled, they have a dark vertical bar extending down from the eye, and no
markings on the dorsal and anal fins. The grass or redfin pickerel has a

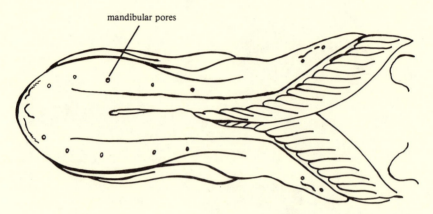

mandibular pores

Figure 14. View of ventral side of jaw showing mandibular pores on northern pike

shorter snout than the chain pickerel and lacks the chainlike markings on the side. The back and sides are olive-green to brown grading to white on the belly. This is overlain by a series of vertical wavy dark green to brown bars.

Life History

All members of the family spawn in the early spring shortly after the ice goes out. Ripe adults move into marshes, flooded meadows or shallow bays to spawn. The eggs are broadcast in water less than two feet deep, each female producing between 750 and 4,600 eggs. The female also carries a second set of later maturing eggs which may be spawned in the fall. No parental care is given to the young since the adults leave the marsh after spawning. The young grow rapidly, feeding on zooplankton initially, and then insects, and eventually small fish. They are sight feeders, feeding only in the day. Grass or redfin pickerel live for about 7 years, achieving a length of 10–12 inches. They prefer living in a habitat with a dense stand of submerged aquatic vegetation, usually in slow-moving streams or lakes. In large lakes and rivers they are more commonly found in stream mouths entering the lake or river than in the larger bodies of water themselves.

Grass or redfin pickerel, although not large, are scrappy fish when taken on light gear. The flesh is tasty, but quite bony.

Distribution

Two subspecies of *Esox americanus* are found in New York, *Esox americanus americanus* Gmelin or the redfin pickerel and *Esox americanus vermiculatus* LeSueur or the grass pickerel. The redfin pickerel is primarily a subspecies of the midwest and thus is found in the Alleghany, Lake Erie, Lake Ontario and St. Lawrence drainages in New York. The grass pickerel is an east coast form and primarily known in New York from the Hudson, Delaware and Long Island drainages. They can be distinguished in part by location of capture, but also by the fact that the anal, pectoral, and pelvic fins of the redfin are orange to red in color, whereas in the grass pickerel these same fins are yellowish green.

Other Names

Mud pickerel, grass pike, little pickerel

Chain Pickerel   *Esox niger* LeSueur

Identification

The chain pickerel is distinguishable from the grass or redfin pickerel by the presence of chain-like markings along the side of its body and the longer snout. In addition, if you turn either of the pickerels over and look at the underside of its gill covers you will see a series of slender bones supporting the membranous portion of the edge of the gill cover. These are called branchiostegal rays. The chain pickerel has 14–17, whereas the grass or redfin pickerel has 11–13 branchiostegal rays. The back and sides are olive green to brown grading to white on the belly. The sides are overlain with yellowish-green blotches which cause the darker green background color to form chain-like markings on the sides.

Life History

Chain pickerel spawn in marshy areas and shallow bays shortly after the ice goes out in the spring. Spawning lasts for about 7–10 days, and then the adults leave the spawning grounds. The eggs hatch in 6–12 days and the young reach 4–5 inches by the end of September. They reach sexual maturity at age 3 or 4. They generally fail to live much beyond this age although some individuals have been found which were 8–9 years old. Initially, larval chain pickerel feed on plankton, switching to insects during their first summer, and finally to fish before they are one year old. Most adult chain pickerel are 15–18 inches long and weigh around 1½ pounds. The largest fish caught on hook and line was 13 inches long and weighed 9 pounds, 6 ounces. It was taken in Georgia. In New York the record fish taken by an angler was 6 pounds, 8 ounces, from Harrisburg Lake, Essex County.

Because chain pickerel reach a larger size they are more important to the sport fishery than the grass or redfin pickerel. Unfortunately, few anglers fish specifically for chain pickerel. More commonly pickerel are taken while fishing for bass or pike when the angler is equipped with heavy gear. A better approach would be to go after the chain pickerel with light spinning gear or a fly rod. Any good minnow imitation fished parallel to the edge of a weedbed is bound to bring action and a good fight. The chain pickerel provides a year-round fishery since it is active all year and is readily taken through the ice.

Distribution

The chain pickerel is generally found east of the Appalachians from Nova Scotia south to Florida and west across the Gulf Coast to Texas. In New York the chain pickerel is found in all of the major drainages.

Other Names

Pickerel, grass pickerel, mud pickerel

Northern Pike   *Esox lucius* Linnaeus

Identification

The northern pike lacks scales on the lower half of its operculum as well as the dark vertical bar under its eye, thus separating it from the pickerels. It has light spots on a dark background. The muskellunge, in contrast, has dark spots on a lighter background and no scales on the lower half of either the cheek or operculum. The dark background color of the pike is green to brown. It is darker on the back and shades to a lighter greenish-brown on the sides and eventually to a milky-white belly. The sides are marked with 7–9 horizontal rows of oblong yellowish-green spots.

Life History

Pike spawn early in the spring, shortly after the ice goes off the lakes. They move inshore, seeming to prefer shallow marshes or flooded meadows. They enter the spawning area at night and the run usually lasts 2–3 weeks. Spawning occurs in daylight and begins with a female leading several males slowly around the edge of the marsh in water about a foot deep. Periodically, they line up close to one another, she releases eggs and the males fertilize them. The males often slap the female with their tails at this time, creating an easily discernible commotion for anyone near the marsh. The process continues for several hours until the female has broadcast all of her eggs, which could be as many as 100,000.

The eggs hatch in about two weeks and the young begin feeding on microscopic crustaceans and small insects. It isn't long, however, before they begin feeding on small fish which remain the major part of their diet for the rest of their life.

Pike have been aged, by counting the rings on their scales, that were 24 years old. Some scientists doubt the validity of this technique, so we are unsure how long pike live. They reach sexual maturity at 2 to 5 years. The largest pike reported in North America weighed almost 49 pounds. The largest fish taken by an angler in the United States weighed 46 pounds, 2 ounces, and was taken from New York's Great Sacandaga River in 1940. The average fish caught is closer to 5 or 10 pounds, however.

Pike are found in clear lakes as well as rivers and generally prefer shallow weedy habitats. They are very predaceous, feeding on perch, shiners, frogs, crayfish, and even young waterfowl. They grow to a large size and put up a good fight when hooked. Consequently, they are eagerly sought by sportsmen.

Pike are taken by anglers year round, but seem to be most readily caught in the spring after the spawning run when they are exceptionally hungry. They will strike almost any lure and are readily caught with live minnows as well.

Distribution

The northern pike's range extends in a wide band through the northern portion of North America, Europe, and Asia. In North America its range is from Alaska to Missouri east to the Appalachian Mountains. It is found east of the Appalachians in New England and the Champlain and Hudson drainages. In New York it is found in the Great Lakes–St. Lawrence, Champlain, and Hudson drainages.

Other Names

Pike, great northern pike, pickerel

Muskellunge   *Esox masquinongy* Mitchill

Identification

With no scales on the lower half of either the cheek or operculum; no dark bar below the eye; and a body with dark spots on a lighter background, the muskie is easily separated from other members of the pike family. The back and sides are green to light brown while the belly and undersides are cream. The sides are marked with dark brown or black spots. The color pattern is quite variable, however.

Life History

Spawning occurs in the spring, shortly after the ice melts. Mature adults move into shallow water and marshy areas to spawn normally after northern pike have completed spawning. The spawning behavior is similar to that of the northern pike. Each female lays up to 200,000 eggs. The eggs hatch in 1–3 weeks and the young begin feeding 10 days to two weeks later. For the first few days the young muskie feeds on microscopic crustaceans, but before a week has elapsed, it switches to small fish as a food source. It persists in this habit for the rest of its life, supplementing the fish diet with an occasional salamander, duckling, shrew, or even small muskrat.

Muskies may live up to 20 years and grow to 70 pounds. The average is much less than this. The record muskie for New York and the world, for that matter was taken out of the St. Lawrence River in 1957 and weighed 69 pounds, 15 ounces.

The muskellunge is an important contributor to the sport fishery wherever it is abundant, such as the St. Lawrence River and Chautauqua Lake. Many anglers spend a great deal of time searching for the ultimate angling thrill—the capture of a large muskie.

Distribution

The muskellunge is found only in eastern North America from Ontario and Quebec south to Alabama. In New York it is found in Chautauqua Lake, St. Lawrence River, Lakes Ontario and Erie, Lake Champlain, and the Oswegatchie, and Black drainages.

Other Names

Muskie, maskinonge, lunge

Selected Pike References

Crossman, E. J. 1966. "A Taxonomic Study of *Esox americanus* and Its Subspecies in Eastern North America." *Copeia* 1966(1): 1–20.

Embody, G. C. 1910. "The Ecology, Habits, and Growth of the Pike, *Esox lucius.* Ph.D. thesis, Cornell University. 88 p.

Kleinert, S. J., and D. Mraz. 1966. "Life History of the Grass Pickerel *(Esox americanus vermiculatus)* in Southeastern Wisconsin." *Wis. Conserv. Dep. Tech. Bull.* 37: 40 p.

Oehmcke, A. A., L. Johnson, J. Klingbiel, and C. Wistrom. 1958. "The Wisconsin Muskellunge. Its Life History, Ecology, and Management. *Wis Conserv. Dep. Publ.* 225: 12 p.

Raney, E. C. 1942. "The Summer Food and Habits of the Chain Pickerel *(Esox niger)* of a Small New York Pond." *J. Wildl. Mgt.* 6(1): 58–66.

Threinen, C. W., C. Wistrom, B. Apelgren, and H. Snow. 1966. "The Northern Pike, Its Life History, Ecology, and Management." *Wis. Conserv. Dept. Publ.* 235: 16 p.

Mudminnow   Family Umbridae

Mudminnows are small dark fish with rounded caudal fins. The gas bladder is connected to the esophagus and they are capable of breathing air. They inhabit slow stagnant waters frequently low in oxygen.

Five species comprise the family of which 2 occur in New York.

Species Key

1a. Body marked with thin, dark brown, longitudinal stripes along side. Particularly evident on the lower half of side . . . .
Eastern mudminnow, *Umbra pygmaea.*

1b. Body without stripes, but with faint, vertical bars . . . .
Central mudminnows, *Umbra limi.*

Central Mudminnow   *Umbra limi* (Kirtland)

Identification

There are two species of mudminnows in New York, the central mud-minnow *(Umbra limi)* and eastern mudminnow *(Umbra pygmaea).* Both are small fish, 2–3 inches long, characterized by a rounded caudal fin which is preceded by a distinct dark vertical bar. The central mudminnow is most common and is distinguished from the eastern mudminnow by the absence of horizontal stripes. The dorsal surface of both is olive-green to brown with yellow-brown sides and yellow to white belly. The fins are dark.

Life History

The central mudminnow spawns in March or April, choosing a site in very shallow water with a clean rocky bottom. The female lays 200–2,000 eggs in a natural cavity in the stones, frequently attaching the adhesive eggs to the underside of overhanging rocks or vegetation. She then stands guard over the nest, gently moving her fins, creating a slight current. The male also remains in the area. The nests are usually located in water less than 4 inches deep. The young hatch in about 6 days.

The central mudminnow feeds on ostracods when young and insects, molluscs and larger crustaceans as it becomes older. Some reach sexual maturity in one year, but most reach maturity at two years of age. Rarely do they live beyond four years.

They live in shallow water over a soft bottom, frequently in quite stagnant water. They are very tolerant of low oxygen concentrations. When disturbed they dive into the bottom mud to escape danger, whence the name, mudminnow. Much of their natural habitat is being eliminated due to the draining of wetlands and stagnant marsh areas.

Distribution

The central mudminnow is found primarily in the midwest. It ranges from Lake Champlain and Quebec to Tennessee and Arkansas and north to the Dakotas. In New York the mudminnow can be found in quiet water in the Allegheny, Great Lakes–St. Lawrence, and Hudson drainages.

Other Name

Mudminnow

Selected Mudminnow References

Peckham, R. S., and C. F. Dineen. 1957. "Ecology of the Central Mudminnow, *Umbra limi* (Kirtland)." *Amer. Midland Natur.* 58(1): 222–31.

Westman, J. R. 1941. "A Consideration of Population Life-History Studies in their Relation to the Problems of Fish Management Research, with Special Reference to the Small-Mouthed Bass, *Micropterus dolomieu* Lacepede, the Lake Trout, *Cristivomer namaycush*-(Walbaum), and the Mudminnow, *Umbra limi* (Kirtland)." Ph.D. thesis, Cornell University. 182 p.

Minnow   Family Cyprinidae

The minnows are, for the most part, small fishes. The carp is an obvious exception. Minnows have cycloid scales, soft rays supporting their fins, toothless jaws, and some possess barbels. Many species develop nuptial tubercles during the breeding season. Some species are herbivorous.

This is one of the largest families of fish, with more than 1,600 described species. Almost 50 species are found in New York. We shall discuss only the more abundant and important of them.

Species Key

1a. Dorsal fin elongate containing more than 12 rays 2

1b. Dorsal fin shorter containing fewer than 12 rays (minnows) 3

2a. Upper jaw with 2 fleshy barbels on each side . . . . Carp,
                                             Cyprinus carpio

2b. Upper jaw with no barbels . . . . Goldfish, *Carassius auratus*

3a. Lower jaw containing a cartilaginous ridge in front of lip and separated by a definite groove from lip (Figure 15); basic coloration light brown; no distinct lateral band or caudal spot; peritoneum black; intestine wound around swimbladder . . . .
Stoneroller, *Campostoma anomalum*

3b. Lower jaw without a cartilaginous ridge which is separated by a groove from lip; coloration variable; peritoneum silvery in most, black in *Pimephales*; intestine not wound around swim bladder 4

4a. Barbels present at or near posterior tip of maxillary (sometimes hidden in groove) 5

4b. Barbels absent 15

5a. Premaxillaries nonprotractile (upper lip connected to skin of snout by a bridge of fleshy tissue which interrupts the premaxillary groove) (Figure 16); barbel at tip of maxillary (Figure 17) 6

5b. Premaxillaries protractile (snout and upper lip separated by a groove) (Figure 16); barbel either at tip of maxillary or in advance of tip of maxillary, sometimes concealed in groove (Figure 17) 7

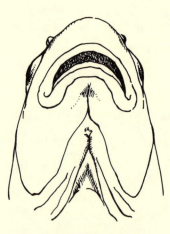

Figure 15. Lower jaw of stoneroller showing cartilaginous ridge

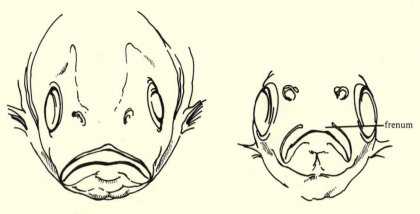

protractile premaxillary   nonprotractile premaxillary

Figure 16. Protractile and non-protractile premaxillaries. In the protractile condition the upper lip is separated from the snout by a groove. In the non-protractile condition this groove is bridged by a frenum.

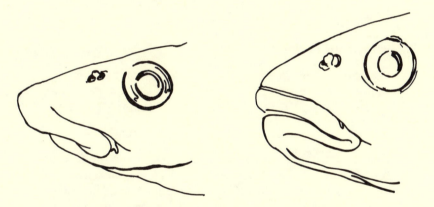

barbel at tip of maxillary   barbel in advance of tip of maxillary

Figure 17. Location of barbel at tip of maxillary and in advance of tip of maxillary

6a. Snout projects far beyond the horizontal mouth (Figure 18); dark lateral band indistinct fusing with basic coloration of side; dorsal fin forward (base of first ray in advance of midpoint of line extending from caudal base to anterior edge of eye) . . . .
Longnose dace, Rhinichthys cataractae

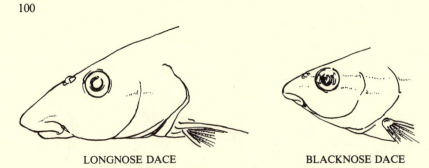

LONGNOSE DACE   BLACKNOSE DACE

Figure 18. Snout of *Rhinichthys*

6b. Snout projects only slightly, if at all, beyond the oblique mouth; (Figure 18) distinct dark lateral band; dorsal fin not forward (base of fins and ray approximately at midpoint of line extending from caudal base to anterior edge of eye) . . . .
Blacknose dace, *Rhinichtys atratulus*

7a. Barbel in groove above maxillary and forward of tip of maxillary (sometimes hard to see in small specimens) 8

7b. Barbel at tip of maxillary 10

8a. Posterior end of upper jaw does not reach as far back as forward edge of eye, mottled coloration . . . . Pearl dace,
Semotilus margarita

8b. Posterior end of upper jaw reaches at least to front of eye 9

9a. Base of first ray of dorsal fin directly over pelvic fin base; no black spot on dorsal base; scales on dorsal midline anterior to dorsal fin of normal size (21–23 scales from base of first ray of dorsal fin to back of head) . . . . . . Fallfish, *Semotilus corporalis*

9b. Base of first ray of dorsal fin just posterior to pelvic fin base; conspicuous black spot on dorsal base; scales on dorsal midline anterior to dorsal fin markedly smaller than other scales on body (35–40 scales from base of first ray of dorsal fin to back of head) . . . . Creek chub, *Semotilus atromaculatus*

10a. Scales small, lateral line scale count more than 50 . . Lake chub,
Couesius plumbeus

10b. Scales larger, less than 50 in lateral line 11

11a. Eye small, its diameter less than length of upper jaw; snout extending only slightly beyond upper lip 12

11b. Eye large, its diameter equal to or greater than length of upper jaw; snout extending a noticeable distance beyond upper lip 13

12a. Large distinct caudal spot; snout length contained more than 9 times in standard length .... Hornyhead chub, *Nocomis biguttatus*

12b. No distinct caudal spot; snout length contained 8 or less times in standard length .... River chub, *Nocomis micropogon*

13a. Body decorated with 7–11 distinct black spots arrayed along lateral line .... Streamline chub, *Hybopsis dissimilis*

13b. Body without spots arrayed along lateral line 14

14a. Origin of dorsal fin over or behind origin of pelvic fin; dark lateral band extending along sides and onto snout .... Bigeye chub, *Hybopsis amblops*

14b. Origin of dorsal fin anterior to origin of pelvic fin; no dark lateral band .... Silver chub, *Hybopsis storeriana*

15a. Lower jaw appearing somewhat deformed, composed of 3 lobes .... a large medial lobe and smaller lateral lobes (Figure 19) 16

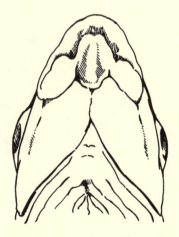

Figure 19. Lower jaw of cutlips minnow showing 3 lobes

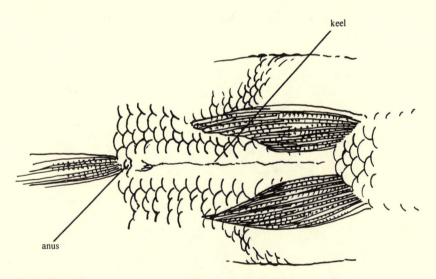

Figure 20. Ventral side of golden shiner showing fleshy, unscaled keel running anteriorly from anus

20a. Angle of mouth reaches to or beyond forward edge of eye.......21

20b. Angle of mouth does not reach forward edge of eye ....
Southern redbelly dace, *Phoxinus erythrogaster*

21a. A dark stripe between lateral band and back ....
Northern redbelly dace, *Phoxinus eos*

21b. No dark stripe between lateral band and back, uniformly pigmented.................Finescale dace, *Phoxinus neogaeus*

22a. First obvious dorsal ray somewhat thickened and separated
from next posterior ray by a membrane; scales small and
crowded on the flattened predorsal region (Figure 21) 23

22b. First obvious dorsal ray a thin splint closely attached to next
posterior ray (Figure 21); predorsal scales more or less normal ...24

23a. Mouth horizontal and not extending as far forward as tip of
snout; (Figure 22) spot at base of caudal fin conspicuous; complete lateral line ...... Bluntnose minnow, *Pimephales notatus*

23b. Mouth oblique and extending as far forward as tip of snout
(Figure 22); spot at base of caudal fin faint; incomplete lateral
line.................Fathead minnow, *Pimephales promelas*

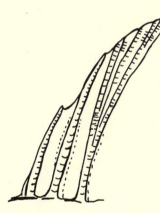

Pimephales   *Notropis*

Figure 21. First obvious dorsal ray of *Pimephales* and *Notropis* showing the sepa-
ration between the first half ray and the first fully developed ray

BLUNTNOSE MINNOW   FATHEAD MINNOW

Figure 22. Lateral view of head of bluntnose and fathead minnow showing shape of mouth

24a. Intestine short, less than twice the length of the head and body; peritoneum silvery; rarely brown or black (Genus Notropis*) 26

24b. Intestine long, more than twice the length of the head and body; peritoneum black 25

25a. Yellowish color; 20 radii on scales . . . . Brassy minnow, *Hybognathus hankinsoni*

25b. Silvery color; 10 radii on scales . . . . Silvery minnow, *Hybognathus nuchalis*

26a. Nine fully developed rays in dorsal fin . . . . . . Pugnose minnow, *Notropis emiliae*

26b. Fully developed rays in dorsal fin 8 27

27a. Anal rays 7 28

27b. Anal rays 8 or more 30

28a. Lateral line incomplete; dark lateral band extends along flanks and across snout . . . . Bridle shiner, *Notropis bifrenatus*

28b. Lateral line complete; no lateral band, or if present does not extend onto snout 29

29a. Dark lateral band present on sides and extending beyond midpoint of body . . . . Swallowtail shiner, *Notropis procne*

*The genus Notropis is composed of a group of about 20 species in New York that are somewhat difficult to identify. For interested students references should also be made to: Eddy (1969), Hubbs and Lagler (1964), Scott and Crossman (1973), or Trautman (1957).

29b. Dark lateral band poorly developed, if present darkest posteriorly and fading as it passes midpoint of body . . . . Sand shiner, *Notropis stramineus*

30a. Anal rays 8 31

30b. Anal rays 9 or more 38

31a. Dark spots on the membranes between the posterior rays of the dorsal fin; diameter of eye goes into head length 4 or more times . . . . Spotfin shiner, *Notropis spilopterus*

31b. No dark spots on the membranes of dorsal fin; diameter of eye goes into head length less than 4 times 32

32a. Dark spot at base of caudal fin . . . . Spottail shiner, *Notropis hudsonius*

32b. No dark spot at base of caudal fin or if present broadly confluent with dark lateral band 33

33a. A black lateral band which extends around head and onto snout present; lateral line incomplete (except for pugnose shiner) 34

33b. Lateral band, if present, dusky and not extending across head and onto snout; lateral line complete 37

34a. Mouth small and nearly vertical, upper jaw extends only as far back as nostril . . . . Pugnose shiner, *Notropis anogenus*

34b. Mouth larger and generally horizontal, upper jaw extends beyond nostril 35

35a. Dark lateral band on snout does not include tip of chin, chin is not black . . . . Blacknose shiner, *Notropis heterolepis*

35b. Dark lateral band on snout includes tip of chin, creating black mark on chin 36

36a. Anterior half of lateral band appears zigzag-like . . . . Blackchin shiner, *Notropis heterodon*

36b. Anterior half of lateral band uniform, without zigzags . . . . Ironcolor shiner, *Notropis chalybeus*

37a. Mouth small, upper jaw about as long as diameter of eye; fewer than 16 predorsal scales . . . . . Mimic shiner, *Notropis volucellus*

37b. Mouth large, upper jaw longer than diameter of eye; more than 16 predorsal scales . . . . Bigmouth shiner, *Notropis dorsalis*

106

46b. Heavier bodied fish with pale green coloration ....
Comely shiner, *Notropis amoenus*

47a. Anal rays 13 or more; common.............. Golden shiner,
Notemigonus crysoleucas

47b. Anal rays 12 or less; uncommon, introduced into lower Hudson
drainage .... Rudd, *Scardinius erythrophthalmus*

Carp   *Cyprinus carpio* Linnaeus

Identification

The carp is one of the easiest members of the minnow family to recognize. Its large size, long dorsal fin, and two pairs of barbels around its
mouth prevent you from confusing it with any other New York fish. It is
olive-green or brown on its back grading to silvery-white on its belly.

Life History

Carp spawn in late May or early June after the water has warmed to
62 or 63°F. Adults move into water so shallow that sometimes their backs
and fins protrude into the air, thus creating a great deal of splashing and
commotion as they go about their nuptial activities. They are easily no-
ticed at a distance during this time, but are very wary and difficult to approach. Carp do not build nests or care for their eggs in any way, they
simply broadcast their eggs over vegetation on the bottom. Consequently,
the eggs suffer a high mortality and, to compensate, females are very fe-
cund. Females carrying more than 2 million eggs have been found. The
eggs hatch in 2–8 days, depending on water temperature, and the young
quickly disperse. Carp fry feed initially on zooplankton, but soon switch
to feeding off the bottom. When bottom feeding they draw material up
into the mouth, spit it out and then pick out any tasty morsels that suit
them. Carp are omnivorous in their feeding habits, consuming both plant
and animal material.

Carp are quite long lived. There is a report of one individual that lived
for 47 years in captivity. In nature, it is unlikely that many individuals exceed a life of 20 years or a size in excess of 40 pounds. The record fish
caught by an angler in New York is 35 pounds, 4 ounces, from Keuka
Lake.

As young fish, carp are quite susceptible to predation. However, after they reach adult size, they are relatively free of predators. They are too large to be killed and eaten by most other fish. Their thick heavy scales provide protection from lamprey attack. The only significant predators are humans.

The carp is one species that is clearly underexploited by the state's fishermen. It is a sturdy fish, tolerant of polluted conditions, that would be able to make use of water that is uninhabitable by other game fish such as trout, pike or bass. It reaches large size and puts up a strong, if not spectacular fight when hooked. Its flesh is tasty when properly prepared. In Asia and Europe the carp is considered such a fine food fish that it is cultured in ponds and sold to fish markets.

Distribution

Carp were originally found in Asia and Europe. The first reported introduction of carp in North America was in a private pond near Newburgh, N.Y., and subsequently into the Hudson River around 1831 or 1832. The U.S. Fish Commission encouraged their introduction throughout the country in the latter part of the 19th century so that now they are widespread throughout the United States and Canada. In New York carp are found in all drainage systems.

Other Names

German carp, European carp

Stoneroller *Campostoma anomalum* (Rafinesque)

Identification

The stoneroller can be recognized by the cartilaginous ridge on the lower jaw. This ridge essentially replaces the lower lip, although vestiges of the lip can still be seen. Another interesting characteristic is the fact that its intestine is coiled around its gas bladder, a trait not shared by other New York minnows. The back is olive-green to brown grading through lighter shades to white on the belly. The fins are yellow-green, the dorsal fin has a dark horizontal band dividing it. During breeding season the dorsal and anal fins develop an orange color.

Life History

Stonerollers spawn from mid-April to June in New York. Males move upstream to small tributaries with good current and a gravel or sand bottom. They are covered, particularly on the back and head, with nuptial tubercles. If you pick one up at this time he will feel almost like coarse sandpaper. As soon as the male finds a suitable site, he begins to build a nest. He pushes and rolls stones out of the nest until he has created a small depression in the gravel. It is this rolling of stones out of the nest that may have given rise to the common name—stoneroller. A female soon joins the male. They spawn over the nest and the heavy eggs sink to the bottom where they will hatch in about three days. After spawning the adults drop back downstream to deeper water.

Stonerollers scrape material off the rocks on the stream bottom, consuming diatoms, algae, microscopic animals of various sorts, and insects in the process. They live up to 5 years and reach 6–8 inches total length.

In some areas stonerollers are used as bait minnows. They are hardy and remain lively on the hook for a long time. They are also interesting to watch in small streams in the spring as they go through their nest building and spawning behavior.

Distribution

The stoneroller is found from the east coast west to Minnesota and Texas. In New York it is found in the Great Lakes–St. Lawrence drainage, as well as the Allegheny and Susquehana drainages.

Other Names

Stone-roller minnow, dough belly

Golden Shiner   *Notemigonus crysoleucas* (Mitchill)

Identification

The golden shiner lacks barbels, has a scaleless, fleshy keel running along the midline of the abdomen to the pelvic fins, and as an adult presents a distinctive golden color. It is a rather deep-bodied fish. The young, silvery and having a distinct dark lateral band running along their sides, are easily confused with shiners (*Notropis*), except that they possess a fleshy keel.

Life History

Spawning occurs from May to August in New York in ponds and lakes. No nest is built; the eggs are simply broadcast over aquatic vegetation and abandoned. The eggs are adhesive and remain attached to the vegetation until the young hatch and disperse. Golden shiners feed on zooplankton, phytoplankton, and small insects. If growth is rapid, they may be ready to spawn in their second summer, otherwise they usually spawn in their third summer. Golden shiners may reach 10 inches in length and live for 8 or 9 years.

Golden shiners prefer relatively clear quiet water with a great deal of aquatic vegetation. They are found in lakes and ponds, or large slow flowing streams and rivers. They generally swim in large schools, feeding at the surface on insects or in midwater on plankton.

A substantial bait fish industry has grown up around this species. It is one of the most important bait species in the state. It is cultured in ponds and sold to anglers. In addition, it is a valuable forage species for lake-dwelling game fish.

Distribution

The golden shiner is found throughout eastern North America from the Maritime Provinces of Canada to Florida and west to North Dakota and Texas. It has been introduced in various parts of western North America as well. It is found throughout New York.

Other Names

Roach, bream, chub, gudgeon, goldfish

Blacknose Dace   *Rhinichthys atratulus* (Hermann)

Identification

The presence of one barbel at the posterior tip of each maxillary and nonprotractile premaxillaries distinguishes the blacknose and longnose daces (Genus *Rhinichthys*) from the other minnows. The snout of the blacknose dace does not protrude much beyond the mouth; whereas it protrudes considerably in the longnose dace (see Figure 18). The blacknose dace is dark olive-green to brown grading to white on its underside. A dark lateral band runs from the tail, along its side, and onto its head. During breeding season the males develop a rusty tinge to their fins.

Life History

Spawning occurs in late May or early June in New York. The adults simply drop the fertilized eggs over the gravel stream bottom without preparing any nest. However, one subspecies, *R. atratulus meleagris*, defends spawning territories vigorously. Females carry around 750 eggs. Blacknose dace are short lived, probably not living for more than 2–3 years, and small adults are usually only 2–3 inches long.

The blacknose dace is a stream dweller, preferring small streams with a steep gradient. It is more commonly found in the quieter parts of these streams than its close relative the longnose dace. Blacknose dace feed on insect larvae, small crustaceans, small worms, and plant material. It is one of the few species found in small headwater streams with brook trout.

Distribution

The blacknose dace ranges from Nova Scotia to Georgia and west to Mississippi and the Dakotas. In New York it is found in all watersheds of the state with the exception of Long Island.

Other Names

Black-nose dace, dace, redfin dace, brook minnow, potbelly

Longnose Dace *Rhinichthys cataractae* (Valenciennes)

Identification

The longnose dace has all of the characteristics outlined for the blacknose except that its snout projects considerably beyond the mouth (see Figure 18). It is olive-green to dark-brown on its back grading to white on the undersides. The sides are somewhat mottled.

Life History

Little is known about the spawning behavior of this species. It is presumed to spawn in late spring or early summer in the gravelly riffle areas where it makes its home. The young are thought to be pelagic, living in still water, near shore. This habit lasts for about 4 months, quite unlike the behavior of the adults, who are bottom dwellers, hugging the bottom in riffle areas of the stream. The species is also found near shore in the rocky areas of large lakes.

Longnose dace live up to 5 years and reach 4–5 inches in length. They appear to live a little longer and achieve slightly larger size than the blacknose dace. They feed primarily on aquatic insect larvae and are considered particularly useful in reducing blackfly populations—a trait which should endear them to any outdoorsman.

Distribution

The longnose is found from coast to coast in central North America, ranging south to Virginia and Mexico and north to Hudson Bay and the Northwest Territories. In New York it is found in all drainages with the single exception of Long Island.

Cutlips Minnow — *Exoglossum maxillingua* (LeSueur)

Identification

The cutlips minnow is easily identified when in hand. Simply look at the lower jaw, which is composed of 3 distinct lobes (Figure 19). No other fish in the state, except for the tongue-tied chub (*Exoglossum laurae*) in the Allegheny drainage has a lower jaw that resembles this. The cutlips is dusky olive-green dorsally and grades to a very light green or cream below.

Life History

Cutlips spawn from mid-May to mid-June with most activity occurring in June. Males construct a nest by carrying carefully selected stones to the nest site and arranging them into a mound 1–1½ feet in diameter and 3–6 inches high. The nest is flat on top. The site chosen for the nest is usually in current and under some form of overhanging shelter. Spawning occurs on the upstream slope of the nest and the eggs are lodged in the gravel nest by the current. The young hatch and leave the nest in 6 days.

Cutlips feed on material taken from the bottom of the clear, gravelly streams they inhabit. Insects and molluscs dominate their diet.

Distribution

The cutlips is found from the St. Lawrence River and eastern Lake Ontario drainages south to Virginia. In New York it is found in all of the major drainages except the Allegheny, Lake Erie, and Long Island.

Other Name

Eye-picker

Fallfish   *Semotilus corporalis* (Mitchill)

Identification

Both the fallfish and the creek chub are easily recognized by the barbel on the maxillary. The barbel is located up from the tip of the maxillary and is thus sometimes hidden in the groove between the maxillary and the snout. Open the mouth and the barbel should be easily seen. If you run a straight line dorsally from the base of the pelvic fin, the origin of the dorsal fin will lie on this line or slightly in front of it, never behind. If it lies behind, the fish is either the creek chub or the pearl dace (*Semotilus margarita*). The fallfish has an olive-brown back, silvery sides, and white ventral surface.

Life History

Fallfish are spring spawners, usually choosing May as the time for their nuptial activities. They prefer quiet water in streams or around the shores of lakes where there is a clean gravel bottom. The male constructs one of the more spectacular nests among the fishes of New York. He picks up small stones and pebbles with his mouth and carries them to the nest site, piling them into a substantial elongate mound. The nest may reach six feet in length and three feet in height. One male spawns over the nest with one or more females, each of which carry about 2,000 eggs. The eggs apparently fall into the interstices between the pebbles in the nest. Little is known of the early development of the fallfish. Young fish prefer the swifter shallower water of a stream in contrast to the adults who remain in deeper quieter water. Little is known of their feeding habits, either, but insects undoubtedly play a major role in their diet.

Fallfish are the largest native freshwater minnows in New York, exceeded in size only by the introduced carp and goldfish. Fallfish have been taken which were nearly 18 inches long and 2 pounds in weight. The typical fish will be closer to 8–12 inches long, however. They have been known to live up to 6 years.

Fallfish readily take a fly. Because of this fact and their substantial size, they have provided sport for many fishermen unable to find trout. Their flesh is good to eat and they put up a strong, though not spectacular fight. The main drawback to a fallfish sport fishery is that few anglers like to admit they fish for minnows.

Distribution

The fallfish is found from New Brunswick to Ontario south to Virginia. In New York it is found in all drainages save the Allegheny, Genesee, Erie, and Long Island.

Other Names

Windfish, silver chub

Creek Chub   *Semotilus atromaculatus* (Mitchill)

Identification

The creek chub, with the barbel up from the tip of the maxillary, as in the fallfish, and the dorsal fin originating behind the origin of the pelvic, is easily distinguished from all other minnows except the pearl dace (*Semotilus margarita*). The pearl dace, however, has a small mouth that does not reach the anterior edge of the eye, whereas the creek chub's mouth is large, reaching at least to the forward margin of the eye. In addition, in adult creek chubs a dark spot is present at the origin of the dorsal fin. The back is olive-green, the sides silvery-white, and the belly white.

Life History

Creek chubs spawn in small streams in the spring. They build nests from gravel found on the bottom at the nesting site. The male picks up small stones and pebbles with his mouth and moves them a short distance upstream. He thereby excavates a pit downstream from a mound of gravel. He continues working downstream until he has created a long mound of gravel about a foot wide and several feet long which parallels the current. At the downstream end of this mound is a pit which will be used for spawning. The male defends this nest from other males in the region. Before long a female enters the pit and the male joins her. The male then performs one of the more interesting spawning acts found among our fishes. While resting next to her, head to head, and tail to tail, he slips his pectoral fin under her body and with the combined effort of his head and pectoral fin he flips her up into a vertical position as if she were standing on her tail. He then wraps himself around her; the two emit eggs and sperm. The female then drifts downstream, belly up, as if dead. All this takes less than a second to accomplish. The female quickly recovers and returns to this nest or another nest to continue spawning until her complement of 3,000-4,000 eggs is exhausted. The male covers the eggs with gravel and then abandons the nest. Little is known of the early life history of the creek chub.

Creek chubs 7 years old have been collected in New York. They can reach 10 inches or more in length, but are more commonly 4-6 inches long. They feed on a wide variety of foods including insects, small fish, and a substantial amount of plant material. Creek chubs, as their name implies, are primarily inhabitants of streams. However, they are occasionally found in small lakes as well.

Creek chubs will take flies or bait and have probably started many small boys on their way to becoming avid anglers. The creek chub is an important bait minnow. It is sturdy and remains lively on the hook for a considerable length of time. When used as bait they are normally collected by the bait dealer from local streams. However, some work is being done on developing techniques to raise creek chubs artificially.

Distribution

The creek chub is found from the Maritime Provinces of Canada west to Montana and south to Texas and Georgia. In New York it is found throughout the state, with the exception of Long Island.

Other Names

Horned dace, chub

Bluntnose Minnow   *Pimephales notatus* (Rafinesque)

Identification

The bluntnose has no barbels, no fleshy keel along the midline of its abdomen, a normal lower jaw, and a dark spot at the base of the first dorsal ray. The creek chub also has the dark spot at the base of the first dorsal ray, but it has a pair of barbels. The first dorsal ray of the male bluntnose is thickened and separated from the second dorsal ray by a membrane. The shiners (*Notropis*) have a thin splint-like first dorsal ray closely pressed against the second dorsal ray. The young bluntnose and the females resemble shiners more in this character. However, they can be separated from shiners by the fact that the scales on the back in front of the dorsal fin are crowded and irregularly arranged. The bluntnose can be distinguished from the fathead minnow by the fact that its mouth is horizontal and is overhung by the snout. In addition, the bluntnose has a conspicuous spot at the base of the caudal fn and a complete lateral line. Its body is olive-green to brown on the back grading to silvery-white on the belly. A dark lateral band extends from the snout to the caudal spot.

Life History

The bluntnose begins to spawn in May or June, waiting until the water temperature reaches 68°F. Intermittent spawning may occur throughout the summer. It spawns in still water, excavating a depression under a flat rock or board. The male builds the nest and defends it. The unusual feature of the bluntnose's spawning behavior is that when the female lays her eggs in the nest she does not deposit them in the bottom, but rather on the underside of the board or flat stone that forms the roof of the nest. The eggs are adhesive and stick to the board or rock. They are laid one or two layers thick and in a patch 4 or 5 inches in diameter, composed of 200–500 eggs. The male guards the nest and tends the eggs, frequently rubbing them with a thick fatty pad that grows on the back of his head apparently for that purpose. If he is removed, the eggs die in less than a day. The eggs normally hatch in one or two weeks. The adults may spawn more than once during the year. The bluntnose usually chooses to spawn in shallow water near shore and is thus easily observed. In fact, you can provide spawning sites for this interesting fish by laying empty flower pots on their side in an area where you suspect bluntnose minnows to occur. Many hours of enjoyable watching can result from this simple expedient.

Food of the bluntnose is about equally divided between plankton and bottom organisms, including benthic diatoms.

The bluntnose is found in clear lakes and ponds and occasionally slow flowing streams and may reach 3 years of age and 3 inches in length.

The bluntnose is an important forage species and is widely used as a bait minnow. It is easily cultured, adapting to flat boards as breeding sites.

Distribution

The bluntnose is found from the Lake Champlain drainage west through the Great Lakes and south to the Gulf states and Virginia. In New York it is found in all drainages except Long Island.

Fathead Minnow   *Pimephales promelas* (Rafinesque)

Identification

The fathead shares most of the characteristics of the bluntnose, except that its mouth is somewhat oblique and is not overhung by the snout. In addition, it has only a very faint spot at the base of the caudal fin and has an incomplete lateral line. The fathead's coloration is olive on the back, grading to white on the belly. In the spring males develop a nuptial coloration that is quite striking. The head becomes dark, the body between the gill cover and the pectoral fin is encircled by a yellowish band, this is followed by another dark band. Under the dorsal fin a second light band rings the body, while the remainder of the body remains dark.

Life History

Spawning takes place in late May or June when the water temperature reaches the 60–64°F range. Some individuals may be found spawning throughout the summer. Spawning location and behavior is similar to that of the bluntnose minnow.

Fathead minnows are omnivorous, feeding on insects, crustaceans, algae, and detritus. They are short lived, normally dying after spawning at two years of age. However, if spawning does not occur, they may live longer. Individuals have been kept for 4 years in aquaria at the College of Environmental Science and Forestry at Syracuse. Adult size is 2 or 3 inches, and is often reached at the end of the first growing season.

The fathead minnow is a valuable forage species, and it is cultured in New York for sale as bait.

Distribution

The fathead ranges from New Brunswick to Alberta south to Mexico. In New York it is found in all waters except the Delaware and those on Long Island.

Spottail Shiner   *Notropis hudsonius* (Clinton)

Identification

There are at least 20 species of shiners in New York waters. To the inexperienced they all look pretty much alike. However, they can be distinguished, and I would suggest referring to Hubbs and Lagler (1964), Eddy (1969), Scott and Crossman (1973), or Trautman (1957) for details.

The spottail shiner is easily identified by the dark spot at the base of its caudal fin, and its eight anal rays. Be careful not to confuse it with the bluntnose, which also has a black spot at the base of the caudal fin. Most of the spottail's body is silvery with the back a greenish-gray and the belly white.

Life History

Spawning takes place in June or early July, when the fish gather in aggregations over a sandy bottom. There is no evidence of nest building. Each female carries 1,300–2,600 eggs. The young begin life by feeding on microscopic algae and rotifers. Later they transfer to small crustaceans, insects, molluscs, and even small fish. They live for 3–4 years and reach a length of 4 inches or more.

The spottail prefers clear water with little turbidity and is generally found in large rivers or lakes with a sand or gravel bottom which are 3–60 feet deep.

The spottail is often used as bait and is an important forage species for game fishes.

Distribution

The spottail shiner is found in a region from the Lake Champlain drainage northwestward to the Northwest Territories and south to Missouri and Georgia. In New York it is found in all waters except the Raquette drainage and Long Island.

Other Name

Spottail minnow

Common Shiner   *Notropis cornutus* (Mitchill)

Identification

The common shiner has a fairly stout body and 9 anal rays. Its dorsal fin has its origin in front of or directly above the base of the pelvic fin. During the breeding season its fins are tinged with pink to red, giving rise to the name redfin. The remainder of the body is silvery with an olive-green back.

Life History

Spawning occurs after the water has reached 60–65°F, which is usually in May or June. Males create a rather primitive depression in the gravel bottom of streams near the head of a riffle. They defend the nest area, while the females wait downstream. Eventually a female will enter the nest and lay about 50 eggs, which are fertilized by the male. The eggs drift to the gravel bottom and, being adhesive, attach to the stones. Since females carry around 1,000 eggs they probably repeat the spawning act more than once. Favored food organisms include insects, algae, and aquatic plants. Common shiners may reach 7 or 8 inches in length and live for up to 5 years. They are the largest species of shiner in New York. Common shiners are basically a stream fish, but populations are also known for clear lakes.

The common shiner serves as forage for many game fish. It also is used as bait by fishermen. It is a fairly delicate fish and does not survive well in the bait bucket or on the hook.

Distribution

The common shiner is found from Nova Scotia west to Saskatchewan and south to Kansas and Virginia. In New York it is found in all drainages save Long Island.

Other Name

Redfin shiner

Emerald Shiner   *Notropis atherinoides* (Rafinesque)

Identification

The emerald shiner has 10–13 anal rays, and its dorsal fin base begins posterior to the base of the pelvic fin. Its back is olive to silvery, grading to white ventrally. An emerald band frequently extends from the upper corner of the gill cover, along the side, to the tail.

Life History

Little is known about the spawning behavior of the emerald shiner. They may begin spawning as early as May, and some individuals may spawn as late as August. They grow rapidly, reaching 2 inches by late fall.

Adults may reach 3–4 inches at the end of three years, their normal life span. They live in schools in the open water of large lakes and rivers, feeding on zooplankton and insects. They tend to move toward the surface at night and down into deeper water during the day, a movement pattern which parallels that of their prey.

The emerald shiner is widely used as bait. It also plays an important role as forage for many game fish.

Distribution

This species ranges from the Lake Champlain drainage northwestward to northeastern British Columbia and south through the Mississippi drainage to the Gulf of Mexico. In New York it is found in all drainages except the Delaware, Susquehanna, Allegheny, Raquette, and Long Island.

Other Name

Lake emerald shiner

Selected Minnow References

Cooper, G. P. 1936. "Age and Growth of the Golden Shiner (*Notemigonus crysoleucas auratus*) and Its Suitability for Propagation." *Pap. Mich. Acad. Sci. Arts Lett.* 21: 587–97.

Forney, J. L. 1968. "Raising Bait Fish and Crayfish in New York Ponds." *N.Y. State Coll. Agr. Cornell Ext. Bull.* 986: 31 p.

Gee, J. H., and T. G. Northcote. 1963. "Comparative Ecology of Two Sympatric Species of Dace (*Rhinichthys*) in the Fraser River System, British Columbia." *J. Fish. Res. Board Canada* 20(1): 105–18.

Greeley, J. R. 1930. "A Contribution to the Biology of the Horned Dace, *Semotilus atromaculatus* (Mitchill)." Ph.D. thesis, Cornell University. 114 p.

Hubbs, C. L., and G. P. Cooper. 1936. "Minnows of Michigan." *Cranbrook Inst. Sci. Bull.* 8: 95 p.

McCann, J. A. 1959. "Life History Studies of the Spottail Shiner of Clear Lake, Iowa, with Particular Reference to Some Sampling Problems." *Trans. Amer. Fish. Soc.* 88(4): 336–43.

Miller, R. J. 1964. "Behavior and Ecology of Some North American Cyprinid Fishes." *Amer. Midl. Nat.* 72(2): 313–57.

Raney, E. C. 1940a. "The Breeding Behavior of the Common Shiner, *Notropis cornutus* (Mitchill)." *Zoologica* 25(1): 1–14, 4 pls.

_____. 1940*b*. "Comparison of the Breeding Habits of Two Subspecies of Blacknose Dace, *Rhinichthys atratulus* (Hermann)." *Amer. Midland Natur.* 23(2): 399–403.

Reed, R. J. 1959. "Age, Growth, and Food of the Longnose Dace, *Rhinichthys cataractae*, in Northwestern Pennsylvania." *Copeia* 1959(2): 160–62.

Ryer, R. III. 1938. "Contributions to the Life History of *Notropis cornutus cornutus* (Mitchill)." Master's thesis, Cornell University. 41 p.

Van Duzer, E. M. 1939. "Observations on the Breeding Habits of the Cutlips Minnow, *Exoglossum maxillingua*." *Copeia* 1939(2): 65–75.

Westman, J. R. 1938. "Studies on Reproduction and Growth of the Bluntnosed Minnow, *Hyborhynchus notatus* (Rafinesque)." *Copeia* 1938(2): 57–60.

Sucker   Family Catostomidae

Suckers are soft-rayed fishes, without an adipose fin, barbels, jaw teeth, or a pelvic axillary process. They have scales on the body but none on the head. The lips are usually large and protruding, and the gas bladder is of the physostomous type.

Suckers are commonly confused with minnows, particularly those minnows with downturned mouths. An easy way to distinguish a sucker from a minnow is to look at the placement of the anal fin on the body. If it is far enough posterior that the distance from the base of the first anal ray to the base of the caudal fin is contained more then 2½ times in the distance from the front of the anal fin to the tip of the snout it is a sucker; if less, a minnow (See Figure 7). Carp and goldfish would be classified as suckers using this rule, but they have a large hard spinous ray at the front of the dorsal fin, suckers do not.

Worldwide there are about 58 known species of suckers. In New York approximately 15 species have been recorded. These include the quillbacks (*Carpiodes*) and buffalo (*Ictiobus*), distinguishable by the long dorsal fin containing more than 20 principal soft rays; the chub-suckers (*Erimyzon*) and spotted suckers (*Minytrema*), whose distinctive characteristic is poor development of the lateral line (*Minytrema*) or complete lack of a lateral line (*Erimyzon*); and the redhorses (*Moxostoma*), recognizable by having 50 or fewer scales in their lateral line and a rounded head. The other 2 genera (*Catostomus*) and (*Hypentelium*) found in the state are quite common, and we will discuss them in more detail.

Species Key

1a. Dorsal fin long, containing more than 20 principal rays.........2

1b. Dorsal fin short, containing fewer than 19 principal rays........3

2a. Mouth terminal, upper lip about on a horizontal line with lower margin of eye......... Bigmouth buffalo, *Ictiobus cyprinellus*

2b. Mouth subterminal, upper lip well below lower margin of eye .. Quillback *Carpiodes cyprinus*

3a. Lateral line complete and well developed.....................4

3b. Lateral line incomplete or missing 12

4a. More than 55 scales in lateral line 5

4b. Fewer than 55 scales in lateral line 6

5a. Rounded snout projects only slightly, if at all, beyond tip of upper lip (Figure 23); posterior end of mouth extends back only to nostrils; no reddish lateral band on males in spring; dorsal rays 11–12; fewer than 80 scales in lateral line; scales approximately square without radii in lateral fields............ White sucker, *Catostomus commersoni*

5b. Bulbous snout projects well beyond tip of upper lip (Figure 23); posterior end of mouth extends back beyond nostrils; reddish lateral band on males in spring; dorsal rays 10; more than 80 scales in lateral line, scales oval in outline with radii evenly dispersed.......... Longnose sucker, *Catostomus catostomus*

6a. Head depressed between eyes, orbital rims raised (Figure 24); eye posterior to midpoint of head .... Northern hogsucker, *Hypentelium nigricans*

6b. Head rounded normally between eyes, orbital rims not raised (Figure 24); eye near middle of head .... (Redhorse, *Moxostoma**) 7

*The members of the genus *Moxostoma* are difficult to identify, even by a good ichthyologist. A brief key for their identification has been provided. However, you might want to consult a more detailed discussion of this genus such as: R. E. Jenkins, "Systematic Studies of the Catostomid Fish Tribe Moxostomatini," Ph.D. thesis, Cornell University, 1970, and C. R. Robins and E. C. Raney, "Studies of the Catostomid Fishes of the Genus *Moxostoma*, with Description of Two New Species," *Mem. Agr. Exp. Sta.* 343 (1956).

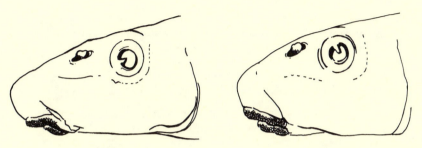

LONGNOSE SUCKER   WHITE SUCKER

Figure 23. Relationship of snout to mouth in longnose and white sucker

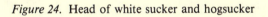

HOGSUCKER   WHITE SUCKER

Figure 24. Head of white sucker and hogsucker

7a. 15 or 16 horizontal scale rows cross an imaginary line describing the circumference of the caudal peduncle at its narrowest point . . . . Greater redhorse, *Moxostoma valenciennesi*

7b. 12 or 13 scale rows cross the circumference of the caudal peduncle at its narrowest point 8

8a. Body depth contained 2.8–3.7 times in standard length; plicae or folds in lips with transverse lines . . . . Silver redhorse, *Moxostoma anisurum*

8b. Body depth contained 3.4–4.7 times in standard length; plicae of lips without transverse lines 9

9a. Forward edge of pelvic fins anterior to an imaginary line drawn down from midpoint of dorsal fin; scale bases dark ....
River redhorse, *Moxostoma carinatum*

9b. Forward edge of base of pelvic fins directly below the midpoint of dorsal fin..10

10a. Lateral line scales 44–47; eye diameter half width of lips at widest point.......... Black redhorse, *Moxostoma duquesnei*

10b. Lateral line scales 40–45; eye diameter 2/3 width of lips at widest point..11

11a. Posterior edge of lower lip forms a definite angle of about 100 degrees; snout very slightly overhangs mouth ....
Golden redhorse, *Moxostoma erythrurum*

11b. Posterior edge of lower lip nearly a straight line; snout definitely overhangs mouth .... Shorthead redhorse, *Moxostoma macrolepidotum*

12a. Lateral line present, but incomplete; black spot at the base of each scale forms row of dotted lines on sides; mouth inferior and horizontal .... Spotted sucker, *Minytrema melanops*

12b. Lateral line absent; distinct dark lateral band in young or irregular blotches in adults; mouth subterminal and oblique.........13

13a. Lateral scale rows 35–37; dorsal rays 11–12 .. Lake chubsucker, *Erimyzon sucetta*

13b. Lateral scale rows 39–41; dorsal rays 9–10 .. Creek chubsucker, *Erimyzon oblongus*

White Sucker   *Catostomus commersoni* (Lacepede)

Identification

The white sucker is distinguishable from all other suckers in the state by the fact that it has only 10–13 soft rays in its dorsal fin and 55–85 scales in its complete lateral line, and its snout projects very little if at all beyond its upper lip. The white sucker is gray to brown on its back, grading to creamy white on its underside.

Life History

White suckers spawn in April or May, moving at night into fast-flowing streams to mate. They seem to prefer gravel bottoms with good current, but some have been reported to spawn in pools or even in lakes. The males develop nuptial tubercles on their anal and caudal fins during the spawning season. Occasionally, females develop small nuptial tubercles, too. A single female may carry up to 140,000 eggs, but the average is much less. After spawning the adults drop downstream, returning to the lake or deeper parts of the stream.

The eggs are adhesive and remain attached to the gravel until hatching, which occurs in 5-10 days. The fry move downstream to deeper water shortly after hatching.

Initially, suckers feed on microcrustaceans, rotifers, and algae; as they grow they feed more commonly on insects, larger crustaceans, snails, and clams. There is no evidence that they feed on eggs of trout or salmon or any other fish for that matter. Since young suckers serve as forage for game fish, they are an asset to the fish community. Suckers appear to be selective in what they eat and do not function as a vacuum cleaner of the bottom.

White suckers rarely reach 10 years of age, although some dwarf varieties have been aged at 18. Adults may reach 18-20 inches and 3-4 pounds. Larger fish than this have been reported, but not commonly.

There are few places in the state where one cannot find white suckers. They are very tolerant of poor environmental conditions, and they are also residents of pristine lakes and streams.

White suckers are not considered a game fish, but they are taken occasionally by trout fishermen. The flesh is not of the highest quality most of the year, but in the spring, during the spawning run, they can provide tasty eating. The only difficulty is the large number of small bones. This problem can be overcome by grinding the meat and preparing fish cakes. In any case, it is poor practice to throw suckers up on the stream bank to allow them to die and rot. They should be treated as other fish, either eaten or returned carefully to the water.

Distribution

The white sucker's range extends from Labrador to the Northwest Territories south to Oklahoma and Georgia. In New York it is found throughout the state other than Long Island.

Other Names

Common sucker, mullet

Longnose Sucker   *Catostomus catostomus* (Forster)

Identification

The longnose sucker deserves its name since the snout projects well beyond the tip of its upper lip. This, plus the fact that it has more than 80 scales in its lateral line, distinguishes it from the white sucker. The back is dark-olive to black, grading to creamy-white on the underside. A coppery tone underlies this basic color pattern. During spawning season a broad lateral band of a rose or wine color develops.

Life History

Longnose suckers spawn in May or June, usually in swift-flowing streams with gravel bottoms. The red lateral band of the male develops more noticeably than does the female's. Unlike the white sucker, the longnose suckers appear to spawn in the day. The female sucker broadcasts 10–60,000 adhesive eggs over the bottom. The eggs hatch and the young leave the stream before they are a half inch long. Upon reaching the lake they stay in shallow weedy areas until they are 2–6 inches long. Eventually they move into deeper water, where the adults are normally found.

Initially, they feed upon plankton, switching to plant material, midge larvae, and amphipods after several weeks. Adults feed heavily on midge larvae.

The oldest fish reported was aged 19 years, but the majority probably do not live beyond 10 years. Most fish are less than 24 inches long and less than 4 pounds in weight.

Distribution

The longnose sucker ranges from Siberia through Alaska and Canada and extends down into the northern part of the United States. In New York it is found primarily in lakes along the northern edge of the state in the Great Lakes–St. Lawrence and Hudson drainages, but it has also been reported from the east and west branches of the Delaware and Long Island.

Other Name

Fine-scale sucker

Northern Hog Sucker *Hypentelium nigricans* (LeSueur)

Identification

If you lay a straightedge across the head connecting the eyes of a hog sucker you will see that the head is depressed under the straightedge. This concavity in the head is the characteristic that distinguishes the hog sucker from the rest of the suckers. The back is olive-brown, grading through light-brown or yellow on the sides to white on the belly. The back and sides are marked with irregular dark blotches.

Life History

Hog suckers spawn in the spring, in April and May, in swift-flowing streams just like the other suckers. After the eggs hatch, however, the hog sucker remains in the stream. It is characteristically a stream fish, preferring clear, swift-moving water. During the winter it drops downstream into deeper areas to spend the winter. When the water temperature rises to about 60°F in the spring they begin to move upstream, searching out rocky riffles for spawning sites.

Food of the hog sucker consists of a variety of bottom insects and crustaceans found in streams. They reach 10–14 inches in length and 1–1½ pounds in weight. Individuals have been found that were 9 years old, but the majority are less than 5 years of age.

Distribution

The hog sucker ranges from southern New York south to Alabama and west to Oklahoma and Minnesota. In New York it is found in Great Lakes–St. Lawrence, Allegheny, Susquehanna, and Hudson drainages.

Other Names

Hammerhead, stoneroller sucker

Selected Sucker References

Bailey, M. M. 1969. "Age, Growth, and Maturity of the Longnose Sucker, *Catostomus catostomus*, of Western Lake Superior." *J. Fish. Res. Bd. Canada* 26: 1289–99.

Dence, W. A. 1948. "Life History, Ecology, and Habits of the Dwarf Sucker, *Catostomus commersoni utawana* (Mather), at the Huntington Wildlife Station." *Roosevelt Wildlife Bull.* 8(4): 81–150.

Raney, E. C., and E. A. Lachner. 1946. "Age, Growth and Habits of the Hog Sucker, *Hypentelium nigricans* (LeSueur), in New York." *Amer. Midland Natur.* 36(1): 76–86.

Raney, E. C., and D. A. Webster. 1942. "The Spring Migration of the Common White Sucker, *Catostomus commersoni* (Lacepede) in Skaneateles Lake and Inlet, New York." *Copeia* 1942(3): 139–48.

Werner, R. G. 1979. "Homing Mechanism of Spawning White Suckers in Wolf Lake, New York." *N.Y. Fish & Game Journal* 26(1): 48–58.

Catfish   Family Ictaluridae

The catfishes are scaleless fishes with flattened heads and a wide mouth surrounded by barbels. The dorsal and pectoral fins are armed with a stout spinous ray which in some species is equipped with a poison gland.

Approximately 37 species are known, all from North America. In New York 9 or possibly 10 species exist. We will discuss only one representative of each of the 3 major groups: bullheads, catfishes, and madtoms.

SPECIES KEY

1a. Adipose fin free at posterior margin, not fused with back and caudal fin (Figure 25); moderate to large fish 2

1b. Adipose fin attached to back and fused with caudal fin, no free end (Figure 25); small fish, usually less than 6 inches 6

2a. Caudal fin slightly rounded, not deeply forked; jaws nearly equal in length 3

2b. Caudal fin distinctly forked; upper jaw noticeably longer than lower jaw 5

3a. Four barbels under jaw predominantly white; anal rays 25–26. .
                         Yellow bullhead, *Ictalurus natalis*

3b. Barbels under jaw gray or black; anal rays 16–24 4

4a. Posterior edge of pectoral spine with stout barbs (grasp pectoral spine between thumb and forefinger with thumb at poste-

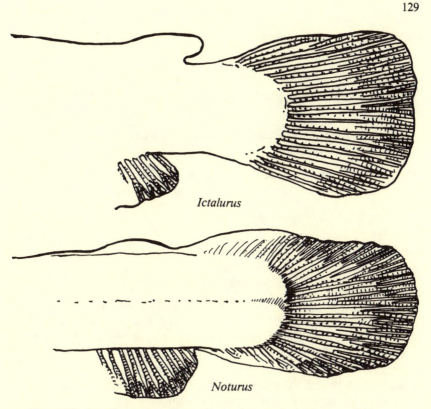

Ictalurus

Noturus

Figure 25. Attachment of adipose fin in the genera *Ictalurus* and *Noturus*

rior edge of spine, pull outward; thumb should be held by barbs); anal rays 22–23 . . . Brown bullhead, *Ictalurus nebulosus*

4b. Posterior edge of pectoral spine without stout barbs; anal rays 17–21 . . . . Black bullhead, *Ictalurus melas*

5a. Body with black spots (more prominent in young individuals, spots fade on fish larger than 12 inches); anal rays 24–30 . . . . . . Channel catfish, *Ictalurus punctatus*

5b. No black spots on body; anal rays 19–23 . . . . White catfish, *Ictalurus catus*

6a. Posterior edge of pectoral spine without barbs or teeth (feels smooth when rubbed with finger) 7

6b. Posterior edge of pectoral spine with strong barbs or teeth 8

7a. Tooth patch in upper jaw (premaxillary teeth) with lateral extensions projecting backward; slender bodied . . . . Stonecat,
Noturus flavus

7b. Premaxillary tooth patch without backward lateral extensions; stocky body . . . . Tadpole madtom, Noturus gyrinus

8a. Length of barbs of pectoral spine does not exceed half diameter of the pectoral spine . . . . . Margined madtom, Noturus insignis

8b. Length of barbs of pectoral spine exceeds half diameter of the pectoral spine . . . . Brindled madtom, Noturus miurus

Brown Bullhead   Ictalurus nebulosus (LeSueur)

Identification

The brown bullhead is readily distinguished by its square to rounded caudal fin, free adipose fin, dark barbels under its jaw, and the large barbs on the inside edge of the pectoral spine. The black bullhead has much smaller barbs on its spines. The yellow bullhead has white barbels under its chin. Coloration of the brown bullhead is quite variable but is basically dark brown to black on the back, grading through gray, green and yellow on the sides, to a yellowish-cream belly.

Life History

Bullheads spawn in late spring or early summer, usually in shallow water after the water temperature has reached 70°F. The male constructs an irregular nest, preferring a site with some shelter such as a log or rock. The nest is cleared by pushing movements of the fish and by lying close to the bottom and actively vibrating the body. Spawning takes place on the nest with the female lying side by side with the male. She will release 2,000–14,000 eggs as a result of several spawning acts. Both parents remain near the nest, one, probably the male, guarding the nest; the other, presumably the female, incubating the eggs. Incubation consists of a rather violent agitation of the eggs by movement of the female's fins and body. If the eggs are removed from the nest and incubated under conditions of flow and oxygen concentration suitable for rearing trout eggs, they die. The only way the eggs can be induced to hatch is to place them in a container in which the flow is strong enough to cause them to be violently agitated. It is thought that the thick gelatinous sheath covering the eggs protects them from mechanical shock, but inhibits oxygen movement to the egg, thus the need for a great deal of agitation. Incubation lasts 5–14 days. The young remain on the nest for a time, developing the characteristic coal black coloration. Eventually they leave the nest, swimming about in a tight aggregation of very black, small bullheads called a pod. The parents swim near the young, acting somewhat like sheep dogs, keeping the pod under control. This is a very characteristic trait of bullheads that can easily be observed in ponds or lakes during the summer since the young fish often swim quite near the surface.

Bullheads that were 6 years old have been caught. It is likely that they may live longer than this. They may grow to 14–16 inches in length and a weight of 1–2 pounds. They are omnivorous, feeding at night with the aid of their barbels. The barbels contain very sensitive chemical receptors which enable the bullhead to locate its prey.

Bullheads are found in lakes and ponds throughout the state. They prefer standing water to flowing streams. During the winter they are known to bury themselves with their mouths protruding from the bottom muds where they remain until the water warms up in the spring.

The bullhead is an excellent food fish. Its flesh is light and tasty, and it is easy to catch. Bullhead fishing is best at night, using live bait such as worms or bits of fish. The bullhead has no scales, so it must be skinned before cooking. It is also one of the more important parts of the catch of commercial fishermen in Lake Ontario.

Distribution

It ranges across southern Canada to the Great Lakes and south to Arkansas and Florida. In New York it is found in every drainage system and is the only freshwater catfish to be found on Long Island.

Other Names

Bullhead, horned pout, common bullhead, speckled bullhead, bullhead catfish

Channel Catfish   *Ictalurus punctatus* (Rafinesque)

Identification

The channel catfish is characterized by a deeply forked caudal fin, a free adipose fin, dark spots scattered along its side in juveniles and females, and 24–30 anal rays. The only other catfish with a deeply forked caudal fin is the white catfish (*Ictalurus catus*) and it has 19–23 anal rays, and no spots. The color of the channel catfish is black to light blue on its back, grading to creamy-white on its belly.

Life History

The spawning behavior of the channel catfish is similar to the brown bullhead except that channel catfish frequently spawn in streams. They also live longer and get much larger; some reaching 24 years of age and 13 pounds. The average, however, is considerably less than this. The New York record is 19 pounds, 10 ounces, recorded from a fish taken in Lake Champlain.

Channel catfish live in large streams, rivers, or lakes with rocky or sandy bottoms. They are not normally associated with heavily vegetated habitat as are the bullheads. They feed at night on all types of aquatic organisms.

The channel catfish is an excellent food fish and, in addition, an excellent sport fish, providing a fine battle when taken from swift water. Currently they are being commercially reared in ponds, particularly in the south for food.

Distribution

Originally this fish was found throughout the central part of the U.S. from Florida north along the western slopes of the Appalachians to Canada, west to Montana, and south to northern Mexico. It has since been introduced east of the Appalachians and westward to California. Channel catfish are found in New York in Lakes Erie, Oneida, and Champlain, as well as large rivers in the Great Lakes drainage.

Other Names

Spotted catfish, silver catfish, lake catfish

Margined Madtom *Noturus insignis* (Richardson)

Identification

The madtoms are easily distinguished from other catfishes in that they are small fish with their adipose fin joined to the back and caudal fin with no free end. Three other species are known for the state, the stonecat (*Noturus flavus*), tadpole madtom (*Noturus gyrinus*), and brindled madtom (*Noturus miurus*). The stonecat has a band of teeth in the upper jaw which runs backward along each side of the jaw. This is not true for the madtoms. The tadpole madtom has no barbs on the posterior margin of its pectoral spine; whereas the margined and brindled madtoms have at least some type of barbs on their pectoral fins. The brindled madtoms barbs are more than half the diameter of their pectoral spine. The margined madtom's barb is less than half the diameter of the spine. The margined madtom is one of the more common madtoms in the state.

Life History

Madtoms spawn in midsummer, probably late June, females producing about 100 eggs. Little is known of their spawning behavior. They reach sexual maturity during their second or third summer and usually live for only 4 or 5 years. They feed on insects and small fish growing to 5–6 inches and 1/10 of a pound.

Distribution

This species is found east of the Allegheny Mountains from Lake Ontario to Georgia. In New York it is found in the Mohawk, Hudson, Delaware, Susquehanna, and Oswego drainages.

Other Names

Madtom, stone bullhead, river bullhead

Selected Catfish References

Clugston, J. P., and E. L. Cooper. 1960. "Growth of the Common Eastern Madtom in Central Pennsylvania." *Copeia* 1960(1): 9–16.

Raney, E. C., and D. A. Webster. 1940. "The Food and Growth of the Young of the Common Bullhead, *Ameiurus nebulosus nebulosus* (LeSueur), in Cayuga Lake, New York." *Trans. Amer. Fish. Soc.* 69(1939): 205–209.

Reed, H. D. 1907. The poison glands of *Noturus* and *Schilbeodes*. *Amer. Natur.* 41(489): 553–66.

Regier, H. A. 1963. "Ecology and Management of Channel Catfish in Farm Ponds in New York." *N.Y. Fish Game J.* 10(2): 170–85.

Taylor, W. R. 1969. "A Revision of the Catfish Genus *Noturus* Rafinesque with an Analysis of Higher Groups in the Ictaluridae." *U.S. Nat. Mus. Bull.* 282: 315 p.

Pirate Perch   **Family Aphredoderidae**

The pirate perch is the only member of this family. It is characterized by the fact that the anus in the adult is located on the throat just posterior to the gill cover. No other species of freshwater fish in the state shares this trait. It is rare or absent throughout most of the state except on Long Island, where it is occasionally found.

Troutperch   Family Percopsidae

The troutperches share characteristics of the soft-rayed fishes and the spiny-rayed fishes. Their scales are ctenoid, the swim bladder is of the physoclistus type, and the dorsal and anal fins are preceded by one or 2 soft spines. They also have an adipose fin.

Only two species are known in this family of which one, the trout-perch *Percopsis omiscomaycus*, is found in New York.

Troutperch   *Percopsis omiscomaycus* (Walbaum)

Identification

The troutperch is a small minnow-like fish, usually less than 5 inches long, with an adipose fin, rough ctenoid scales, and 1–3 very weak spines at the anterior edge of the dorsal fin. The only other fishes in the state with adipose fins are the catfishes, which are easily distinguished by their barbels, and the trouts, salmon, whitefish, and smelt, all of which have smooth cycloid scales and no spines. The background color of the trout-perch is silvery and is overlain with 5 horizontal rows of dark spots on the back and sides.

Life History

Upon reaching one year of age, troutperch leave deep water and move in toward shore or into tributary streams in the spring when the water temperature approaches 68°F. They spawn over rock or gravel sub-strate. Each female carries about 350 eggs. After spawning the young are left to care for themselves.

They feed on crustaceans, zooplankton, and small insects. Most of their total growth is completed before their first winter, when they have reached about 3 inches. They may live up to 4 years, but most do not live beyond the age of 2 years.

Troutperch are found in lakes and slow-moving streams with sandy or gravelly bottoms. They are intolerant of clay bottom habitat. Trout-perch are generally found in very deep water during the day but will some-times come into shallow water to feed at night.

Distribution

This species' range extends from Quebec to Alaska on the north and from West Virginia to Kansas on the south. In New York it is found in the Allegheny, Great Lakes–St. Lawrence, and Hudson drainages.

Other Name

Silver chub

Selected Troutperch References

Kinney, E. C., Jr. 1950. "The Life-History of the Trout Perch *Percopsis omisco-maycus* (Walbaum), in Western Lake Erie." M.S. thesis. Ohio State Univ., Columbus, Ohio. 75 p.

Magnuson, J. L., and L. L. Smith. 1963. "Some Phases of the Life History of the Trout-Perch." *Ecology* 44(1): 83–95.

Burbot   Family Gadidae

Burbot (codfishes) are primarily a group of physoclistus marine fishes of considerable economic importance. Their scales are cycloid, and soft rays support their fins. Members may have 1–3 dorsal fins and 1–2 anal fins.

There are approximately 55 species in this family, of which only one, the burbot *Lota lota*, is truly freshwater. A second species, the tomcod, *Microgadus tomcod*, will occasionally enter freshwater reaches of the Hudson.

Species Key

1a. Dorsal fin divided into two parts; anal fin single . . . . . . Burbot,
Lota lota

1b. Dorsal fin divided into three parts; anal fin divided into two parts . . . . Tomcod, *Microgadus tomcod*

Burbot   *Lota lota* (Linnaeus)

Identification

The burbot is readily distinguished from other species by the presence of a single conspicuous barbel at the tip of the lower jaw. It is the only member of the codfish family found throughout its life cycle in freshwater in New York. Its background color is a yellowish-tan overlain by an irregular network of dark brown markings.

Life History

Burbot spawn under the ice at night in late winter. Frequently, large groups gather and the eggs are broadcast across the sandy bottom of a lake or river and fertilized by accompanying males. The eggs incubate, without benefit of a nest, for 4–5 weeks before hatching. Burbot are very prolific. A single female may produce more than a million eggs; the average fish produces half that number. Burbot mature around 3 years of age, and some individuals are known to live to 16 years. Adult burbot average around 15 inches and weigh ⅔ pound. Some grow considerably larger. The biggest burbot reported in North America was taken in Alaska and weighed almost 60 pounds.

Burbot are deep coldwater fish, found primarily in large lakes and rivers. Young fish will feed on plankton or insects, but as they grow older they feed almost exclusively on other fish such as perch, cisco, or whitefish.

The burbot is often taken by anglers while fishing for other species. Although it may be treated with disdain when caught the burbot is good to eat. It has been considered a highly desirable food fish by Europeans, particularly the Russians, for many years. In America, the appearance of the burbot is presumably sufficient to deter people from eating it.

Distribution

The burbot has a circumpolar distribution. It is found throughout Canada, the northern U.S., Alaska, the Soviet Union, and the Scandinavian countries. In New York it is found in the Allegheny, Great Lakes–St. Lawrence, and Susquehanna drainages.

Other Names

Ling, lawyer, eel-pout, gudgeon

Selected Codfish References

Clemens, H. P. 1951a. "The Food of the Burbot, *Lota lota maculosa* (LeSueur), in Lake Erie." *Trans. Amer. Fish. Soc.* 80(1950): 56–66.

_____. 1951b. "The Growth of the Burbot, *Lota lota maculosa* (LeSueur), in Lake Erie." *Trans. Amer. Fish. Soc.* 80(1950): 163–73.

Robins, C. R., and E. E. Deubler, Jr. 1955. "The Life History and Systematic Status of the Burbot, *Lota lota lacustris* (Walbaum), in the Susquehanna River System." *New York State Mus. Sci. Serv. Circ.* 39: 1–49.

Killifish   **Family Cyprinodontidae**

The killifishes are soft-rayed, physoclistus fishes with cycloid scales. Their mouth appears modified for surface feeding.

Nearly 300 species of killifishes are known, of which only 6 are known for New York.

SPECIES KEY

1a. Teeth notched forming 3 cusps . . . . Sheepshead minnow,
$\qquad$ *Cyprinodon variegatus*

1b. Teeth without cusps, conical 2

2a. Jaw teeth arranged in a single series . . . . Rainwater killifish,
$\qquad$ *Lucania parva*

2b. Jaw teeth arranged in more than one series 3

3a. Base of first dorsal ray is posterior to base of first anal ray . . . . .
$\qquad$ Spotfin killifish, *Fundulus luciae*

3b. Base of first dorsal ray is directly over or slightly in advance of first anal ray 4

4a. Least depth of caudal peduncle contained more than 9 times in standard length . . . . Banded killifish,
$\qquad$ *Fundulus diaphanus*

4b. Least depth of caudal peduncle contained less than 9 times in
standard length 5

5a. Long pointed snout, length 2 times eye length; snout distinctly
below horizontal plane of middle of eye . . . . . . Striped killifish,
Fundulus majalis

5b. Short round snout, length slightly greater than eye length;
snout on a level with or slightly above horizontal plane of middle of eye . . . . Mummichog, *Fundulus heteroclitus*

Banded Killifish   *Fundulus diaphanus* (LeSueur)

Identification

The banded killifish is a small fish with only soft rays supporting its
dorsal fin, a rounded caudal fin, and pelvic fins lying almost entirely in
front of its dorsal fin. There are at least 6 species of killifish that spend
time in freshwater in New York. The most common and widely distributed of these is the banded killifish. The others are brackish water forms
found primarily in estuaries. The back of the banded killifish is olive-
green to brown, the sides pale yellow to white with 12–20 vertical fingers
projecting down from the back. The underside is white.

Life History

The banded killifish may spawn any time from late spring into late
summer. They spawn in extremely shallow, quiet water around the shores
of lakes. They generally choose sites with abundant aquatic vegetation.
The female extrudes a cluster of eggs which remain attached to her genital
papilla by a fine transparent thread. The eggs are immediately fertilized
by an attendant male and then dropped from the female, immediately becoming entangled in the vegetation. Females normally carry no more than
a few hundred eggs.

Banded killifish have a mouth which would seem to be well adapted
to feeding from the water surface. However, studies of the stomach con-
tents of killifish in Canada have shown that they feed on organisms from
a wide variety of different habitats, including a large number of bottom

organisms. Generally, they feed on small insects, crustaceans, and plant material.

Banded killifish grow to a size of 2–3 inches and may spawn at one year of age.

Distribution

This species is found from the Maritime Provinces of Canada south to South Carolina with a westward salient extending through New York and the Great Lakes to Montana. In New York it is found in all drainages.

Other Names

Barred killifish, grayback minnow, topminnow, killy

Selected Killifish References

Richardson, L. R. 1939. "The Spawning Behavior of *Fundulus diaphanus* (Le-Sueur)." *Copeia* 1939(3): 165–67.

Silversides   Family Atherinidae

Silversides are small, slightly elongate, delicate physoclistus fishes with cycloid scales. Their lateral line is greatly reduced or missing.

Approximately 156 species are known, primarily from tropical waters. Only one, the brook silversides, *Labidesthes sicculus*, is known from New York's fresh waters. Another, a brackish water species called the tidewater silversides, *Menidia beryllina*, will occasionally enter fresh water.

SPECIES KEY

1a. Snout length greater than diameter of eye; more than 50 scale rows in body length . . . . Brook silversides, *Labidesthes sicculus*

1b. Snout length less than diameter of eye; fewer than 50 scale rows in body length; brackish water species . . . Tidewater silversides, *Menidia beryllina*

Brook Silversides   *Labidesthes sicculus* (Cope)

Identification

The brook silversides is a slender fish, about 2–4 inches long. It is somewhat transparent with a light green band along its side. It has 2 dorsal fins; the first contains 4 spines and is quite easy to overlook, the second containing rays is easily seen. The anal fin is longer than the second dorsal fin.

Life History

The life history of the brook silversides is quite interesting, in that they live for less than 2 years and in some cases only 13–14 months. Adults gather in large groups in shallow water in the spring when the water temperature approaches 68°F. Males often outnumber females. As females enter the spawning group they are immediately chased by several males, causing the female to leap out of the water. Eventually, one male catches up with her, approaches from the rear, and moves alongside her. When this happens the other males terminate the chase, allowing the first male to spawn with the female. The eggs have a long filament which enables them to stick to any vegetation or rock that the filament touches. The young hatch in a few days and move to open water away from shore. Growth is rapid, and by the end of the first summer most of the fish are nearly adult size. The following summer these fish spawn, the majority dying before winter.

The live just under the surface in lakes and open portions of streams and rivers. They tend to school and will frequently jump out of the water, a habit which has led to the name skipjack. They feed on insects and plankton and serve as forage for game fish. They are not good bait fish since they are very fragile and die quickly upon handling.

Distribution

The range of this species extends from New York to Minnesota and south to Texas and Florida. In New York they are found in the Allegheny, Great Lakes–St. Lawrence, and Mohawk-Hudson drainages.

Other Names

Skipjack, silversides

Selected Silversides References

Hubbs, C. L. 1921. "An Ecological Study of the Life-History of the Freshwater Atherine Fish *Labidesthes sicculus.*" *Ecology* 2(4): 262–76.

Nelson, J. S. 1968. "Life History of the Brook Silverside, *Labidesthes sicculus*, in Crooked Lake, Indiana." *Trans. Amer. Fish. Soc.* 97(3): 293-96.

Stickleback   **Family Gasterosteidae**

Sticklebacks are small physoclistus fishes with a dorsal fin composed characteristically of stout isolated spines. The caudal peduncle is very narrow and the caudal fin is rounded or just slightly forked.

Approximately 8 species belong to the family of which 4 are found in New York.

SPECIES KEY

1a. 9 (8–11) dorsal spines; no bony plates on sides . . . .
Ninespine stickleback, *Pungitius pungitius*

1b. 3–6 dorsal spines; bony plates on sides may or may not be present 2

2a. 3 dorsal spines; bony plates on sides . . . Threespine stickleback,
Gasterosteus aculeatus

2b. 4–6 dorsal spines; no bony plates on sides 3

3a. 4–6 short dorsal spines, length of spines less than eye diameter
. . . . Brook stickleback, *Culaea inconstans*

3b. 4 long dorsal spines, length of spines equal to or greater than eye diameter . . . . Fourspine stickleback, *Apeltes quadracus*

Brook Stickleback   *Culaea inconstans* (Kirtland)

Identification

The brook stickleback is the most common stickleback in the state. It can be distinguished from the rest by the fact that it has the membranes of the lower portion of each gill flap joined across the ventral side of the throat to form a fold. All of the other species known in New York have gill membranes that join the isthmus separately. Additionally, the brook stickleback has 5 short isolated spines in its dorsal fin, although these can range from 4–6. The background color is olive-green dorsally to light-green or cream ventrally. This is overlain by light spotting.

Life History

Sticklebacks are an interesting group of fishes in that the male builds a rather elaborate nest and cares for the young while the female merely provides the eggs and then leaves. Brook sticklebacks spawn in the spring, normally in April or May. The male locates a suitable site, usually containing some erect aquatic vegetation such as reeds or grass, and defends it very aggressively against all intruders. He then begins to construct a nest out of dead grass or filamentous algae, binding the nest together with a sticky secretion derived from his kidney. The nest is round, about the size of a small baseball, and has a single opening. The female enters the opening, deposits about 100–250 eggs and leaves. The male enters and fertilizes the eggs and then stands guard over the nest, fanning it all the while. He remains as a very pugnacious protector of the nest.

Brook sticklebacks are short lived, most reaching only their third birthday. They reach sexual maturity at one year and grow to be about 3 inches in length. They live in weedy brooks or small ponds and are known to feed on insect larvae, particularly mosquitoes. They are quite interesting to watch, particularly during the breeding season.

Distribution

This fish can be found from Maine to Montana, and north to Canada's Northwest Territories and Nova Scotia. In New York it is found in all watersheds except the Delaware and Long Island drainages.

Other Name

Five-spined stickleback

Selected Stickleback References

Reisman, H. M., and T. J. Cade. 1967. "Physiological and Behavioral Aspects of Reproduction in the Brook Stickleback, *Culaea inconstans.*" *Amer. Midland Natur.* 77(2): 257–95.

Winn, H. E. 1960. "Biology of the Brook Stickleback *Eucalia inconstans* (Kirtland)." *Amer. Midland Natur.* 63(2): 424–38.

Sculpin   **Family Cottidae**

Sculpins are small fishes with large flattened heads and spines on the preoperculum, scaleless or with limited patches of reduced ctenoid scales on the body, and bottom-living habits. The family is composed of around 300 species, of which 3 are found in New York.

SPECIES KEY

1a. Dorsal fin separated by a definite gap equal to eye diameter; margin of gill membrane free from isthmus . . Deepwater sculpin, *Myoxocephalus quadricornis*

1b. Dorsal fins barely separated, if at all; margin of gill membrane attached to isthmus 2

2a. Pelvic fin rays 3; anal rays 10–12 . . . . Slimy sculpin, *Cottus cognatus*

2b. Pelvic fin rays 4; anal rays 12–14 . . . . Mottled sculpin, *Cottus bairdi*

Mottled Sculpin   *Cottus bairdi* Girard

Identification

Sculpins are small fish, usually 3–4 inches long, with a large flat head. They are scaleless fish with weak, slender spines in the anterior dorsal fin. Darters, which may be confused with them, have scales. The mottled sculpin can be distinguished from the slimy sculpin since it has 4 soft rays in its pelvic fin. It also has a spine in its pelvic fin, but this is small and closely attached to the large anterior soft ray and thus essentially invisible without dissection. Its color is light to dark brown with darker brown mottling. The undersides are light cream.

Life History

The mottled sculpin spawns in the rapidly flowing water of streams in the spring. The male constructs a small nest under stones or vegetation.

He then chases a female into the nest where she deposits several hundred eggs on the top of its upper surface. The male then fertilizes the eggs and guards the nest until the young begin to feed, which may be more than a month.

The mottled sculpin is found in headwater streams and at the margins of Lakes Ontario and Erie. It prefers rocky or gravelly bottoms and will frequent moderately deep water in lakes.

They are known to feed on algae and insects. There are reports that they also feed on trout eggs. The extent to which they inflict any real damage to trout populations by this practice is unclear. It may be that they feed only on those eggs which are scattered and would have died anyway.

Distribution

The range of the mottled sculpin extends from Labrador south to Georgia, west to the Ozarks, and northwest to Manitoba. It is also found in the Missouri and Columbia River drainages. In New York it is found in the Great Lakes–St. Lawrence, Allegheny, and Susquehanna drainages.

Other Names

Miller's thumb, gudgeon

Slimy Sculpin   *Cottus cognatus* Richardson

Identification

The slimy sculpin resembles the mottled sculpin except that it has 3 rather than 4 pelvic rays. Its color is basically the same.

Life History

It is found in cold streams and along the shore of large cold lakes. Spawning occurs in the spring when the water temperature reaches 40–50° F. Males choose a spawning site as did the mottled sculpin. Females are attracted to the nest where they leave some of their eggs on the underside of an overhanging rock or stick. Females 4 inches long will carry about 1,400 eggs. The male guards the nest until the young leave, which may be more than a month. They feed on small invertebrates and insects off the bottom of the stream or lake. They rarely grow beyond 4 inches.

Distribution

The slimy sculpin's distribution is more northern than the mottled sculpin, extending throughout most of Canada, Alaska, and even Siberia. In the U.S. it is found in the northern tier of states from the Great Lakes drainage eastward. In New York it is found in all major drainages, except Long Island.

Other Names

Miller's thumb, slimy muddler, stargazer

Selected Sculpin References

Koster, W. J. 1936. "The Life History and Ecology of the Sculpins (Cottidae) of Central New York." Ph.D. thesis. Cornell University, Ithaca, N.Y.

_____. 1937. "The Food of Sculpins (Cottidae) in Central New York. *Trans. Amer. Fish. Soc.* 66: 374–82.

Ludwig, G. M., and C. R. Morden. 1969. "Age, Growth, and Reproduction of the Northern Mottled Sculpin (*Cottus bairdi bairdi*) in Mt. Vernon Creek, Wisconsin." *Milwaukee Pub. Mus. Occas. Pap. Natur. Hist.* 2: 67 p.

Savage, T. 1963. "Reproductive Behavior of the Mottled Sculpin, *Cottus bairdi* Girard." *Copeia* 1963(2): 317–25.

Temperate Bass   **Family Percichthyidae**

The temperate basses are moderate to large physoclistus fishes with ctenoid scales and a complete lateral line. Their pelvic fin has one spine and 5 rays; their dorsal is composed of two fins, an anterior spinous dorsal, and a posterior soft dorsal fin.

The family is composed of 40 species of which 3 are found in New York.

Species Key

1a. Spinous dorsal fin slightly joined to soft dorsal; 8–10 soft anal rays; the 3 anal spines not graduated, the second spine is almost as long as the third (Figure 26); lower and upper jaw of same

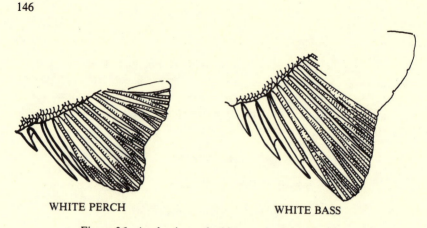

WHITE PERCH   WHITE BASS

Figure 26. Anal spines of white perch and white bass

length; no distinct horizontal lines on sides . . . . . . White perch,
Morone americana

1b. Spinous dorsal separated from soft dorsal; 9–13 soft anal rays;
the 3 anal spines graduated in length, the first about ⅓ the
length and the second about ⅔ the length of the third (Figure
26); lower jaw projects beyond tip of snout; 5–7 dark narrow
lines running horizontally along side of body 2

2a. 12–13 soft anal rays; body depth greater than ½ standard
length . . . . White bass, *Morone chrysops*

2b. 9–11 soft anal rays; body depth less than ⅓ standard length . . .
Striped bass, *Morone saxatilis*

White Bass   *Morone chrysops* (Rafinesque)

Identification

The temperate basses (Percichthyidae) are the only freshwater fishes
in New York with two separate and distinguishable dorsal fins, the anterior spiny and the posterior soft rayed, which also have 3 spines in their
anal fin. The white bass is recognized in the field by the presence of 5–7
dark narrow bands running horizontally along the side of the body. In addition, its lower jaw projects beyond the tip of the snout, thus making it

easy to separate from the white perch. The back is dark green, the sides silvery, and the underside white.

Life History

White bass spawn in May or the first few weeks in June. They occupy shallow shoal areas or shoreline stretches with a gravel or rubble bottom returning to the same spawning grounds year after year. In Wisconsin it has been shown that white bass use the sun as a navigational aid during their migration from deep water to their spawning grounds. Several males accompany each female and as she extrudes eggs near the surface they are fertilized and settle to the bottom where they attach. A female may produce from 25,000 to 1,000,000 eggs, but the mortality rate is high, and very few survive.

The eggs hatch in a couple of days and the fry begin feeding on zooplankton. Their growth is rapid, reaching 4–5 inches by the end of their first summer. They live for 4 or 5 years and reach 14–15 inches and 1–2 pounds. The record for New York is a 2-pound fish caught in Oneida Lake.

White bass prefer large bodies of water (greater than 300 acres) or large rivers with clear water and firm bottoms. They feed on crustaceans, insects, and small fish, including their own young.

Sportsmen are beginning to recognize the angling value of the white bass. It is a schooling species and appears in great abundance in shallow water in the evening. If you encounter a school under these conditions with light tackle you are in for an exciting time. The flesh is light and tasty and the fighting qualities are excellent. White bass can be taken on flies, small spinners, and minnows. One should move quietly around the shallow areas of the lake looking for signs of a feeding school. When spotted, ease up to the school, cast to it, and expect a lot of action.

White bass are taken commercially by fishermen in both Lake Erie and Lake Ontario.

Distribution

The range of the white bass extends from the St. Lawrence River to Lake Huron south through the Mississippi Valley to the Gulf of Mexico. In New York it is found in Lake Erie, Niagara River, Lake Ontario, and the St. Lawrence River as well as Cayuga and Oneida Lakes.

Other Name

Silver bass

White Perch   *Morone americana* (Gmelin)

Identification

The lack of dark horizontal lines on the side and a lower jaw which does not protrude helps to distinguish the white perch from the white bass. The back and base of the median fins are olive green to dark gray, grading to silvery gray on the sides and white on the underside.

Life History

White perch are found in both salt and fresh water; however, they spawn in fresh water, preferring small ponds. They spawn in late spring, producing hundreds of thousands of demersal adhesive eggs. It is thought that the eggs are simply scattered on the bottom and left with no parental care. The eggs usually hatch in less than a week. The species is unusually prolific so much so that even with the haphazard spawning; it is difficult to eliminate a population by overfishing once it is established.

White perch feed on a broad range of food items including minnows, crustaceans, and insects. They travel in schools searching for food and forage over a fairly broad area. Adults are usually less than 10 inches long and one pound in weight. They may live up to 12 years of age.

Angling for white perch offers a double reward: (1) since they travel in schools the action can be fast and furious once a school is found; (2) the meat is deliciously flavored. They are not large fish and will not give you the fight that a large bass or trout would. However, they will bite on almost anything, including dry flies in the evening. So, if you go to light tackle you can have a very enjoyable time with white perch.

Distribution

The white perch is found in coastal waters from the St. Lawrence south to South Carolina. In New York it is found in the Mohawk-Hudson and Long Island drainages. In addition, it has been recently reported from Oneida and Cross Lakes and from Lake Ontario.

Other Name

Silver perch

Striped Bass   *Morone saxatilis* (Walbaum)

Identification

Striped bass characteristically have 7 or 8 dark narrow bands running horizontally the length of the body, 9–11 branched anal rays, and a narrow body whose depth is less than ⅓ standard length. These characteristics plus the fact that striped bass taken in fresh water are large fish (1–10 pounds) will aid in distinguishing striped bass from their close relative, the white bass.

Life History

Striped bass are anadromous and leave salt water to spawn in brackish or freshwater reaches of the Hudson River from Newburgh to Piermont. The spawning season extends from April through June. They prefer to spawn in the river near the mouths of tributary streams. Females normally carry 180,000 to 700,000 eggs, depending on their size. Each female is usually accompanied by several smaller males. The spawning fish swim very close to the surface and, on occasion, will turn on their side and beat the water with their tails, creating a commotion. This has been referred to as a "rock fight." In reality it is the act of spawning. The eggs are semibuoyant and drift with the current until they hatch 2–3 days later. Young striped bass feed on microscopic organisms initially and then quickly graduate to feeding on freshwater shrimp and midge larvae. As adults they feed heavily on small fishes. Late in the summer or early in the fall the young striped bass move downstream to the ocean. Males reach sexual maturity in 2–3 years, females in 4–6 years. Adults normally weigh 1–10 pounds, but fish have been taken that weighed more than 70 pounds. Striped bass may live for 10–12 years, spawning several times during that period.

Striped bass are taken commercially in the Hudson River during the spawning run. They are also taken at sea. The annual commercial catch for all New York fishermen is usually a million pounds or more.

In addition, there is good evidence that the Hudson River is the most northern spawning river for this species. If that is so, it is likely that the majority of the fish taken north of Long Island were derived from Hudson River spawners, thus substantially increasing the economic significance of this spawning population.

A major sport fishery for striped bass exists along the coasts of Long Island. Some fishing for stripers occurs in the Hudson River proper. They are an excellent game fish, achieving large size and exhibiting good fighting qualities.

Distribution

Striped bass are found all along the Atlantic coast from the St. Lawrence River to the St. John's River in Florida. They are also found in the

Gulf of Mexico and have been successfully introduced into Pacific coastal waters of Oregon and California. In New York this fish is found in the lower and middle reaches of the Hudson. It enters the St. Lawrence River, but does not migrate upstream far enough to reach New York.

Other Names

Striper, rockfish

Selected Temperate Bass References

Alsop, R. G., and J. L. Forney. 1962. "Growth and Food of White Perch in Oneida Lake." *N. Y. Fish Game J.* 9(2): 133–36.

Dence, W. A. 1952. "Establishment of White Perch, *Morone americana*, in Central New York." *Copeia* 1952(3): 200–201.

Forney, J.L., and C. B. Taylor. 1963. "Age and Growth of White Bass in Oneida Lake, New York." *N. Y. Fish Game J.* 10(2): 194–200.

Raney, E. C. 1952. "The Life History of the Striped Bass, *Roccus saxatillis* (Walbaum)." *Bull. Bingham Oceanogr. Collect.* 14(1): 5–97.

Sunfish   Family Centrarchidae

Sunfishes are spiny rayed, laterally compressed, physoclistus fishes with the majority possessing ctenoid scales. Their dorsal fin is roughly continuous, and is composed of an anterior spinous portion and a posterior soft-rayed portion.

Thirty species belong to this family of which 14 are found in New York. We will discuss the 7 most common species and leave the 7 rarer species for more detailed accounts.

SPECIES KEY

1a. Caudal fin rounded 2

1b. Caudal fin slightly to distinctly forked 4

2a. Mouth large, maxillary extends posteriorly to middle of eye, cycloid scales . . . . Mud sunfish, *Acantharchus pomotis*

2b. Mouth small, maxillary does not extend to middle of eye; ctenoid scales 3

3a. Opercular spot as large as eye; sides of body with 5-8 distinct dark vertical bands ..... Banded sunfish, *Enneacanthus obesus*

3b. Opercular spot smaller than eye; sides of body with none or indistinct crossbars .... Bluespotted sunfish, *Enneacanthus gloriosus*

4a. Anal spines 5-7; dorsal spines 5-9 or 11-13, rarely 10 5

4b. Anal spines 3; dorsal spines 10 7

5a. Length of base of anal fin about ½ length of dorsal fin base; dorsal spines 11-13 .... Rock bass, *Ambloplites rupestris*

5b. Length of base of anal fin about equal to length of dorsal fin base; dorsal spines 5-9 6

6a. Distance from eye to base of first dorsal spine equal to length of base of dorsal fin; 7-8 dorsal spines; body with irregular dark markings........... Black crappie, *Pomoxis nigromaculatus*

6b. Distance from eye to base of first dorsal spine greater than length of base of dorsal fin; 6 dorsal spines; body pale .... White crappie, *Pomoxis annularis*

7a. Body elongate, its depth contained 3-4½ times in standard length; scales small, more than 55 in lateral line 8

7b. Body deep, its depth contained 2-3 times in standard length; scales large, less than 55 in lateral line 9

8a. Distinct dark band running horizontally along sides of body; notch between two dorsal fins deep, shortest dorsal spine at center of notch contained 2-3 times in length of longest spine (Figure 27); mouth large, end of jaw extends behind posterior margin of eye....... Largemouth bass, *Micropterus salmoides*

8b. Coloration variable, but normally without a distinct lateral band; notch between two dorsal fins not so deep, shortest dorsal spine at center of notch contained 1-2 times in length of longest spine (Figure 27); mouth smaller, end of jaw extends just to posterior end of eye................ Smallmouth bass, *Micropterus dolomieui*

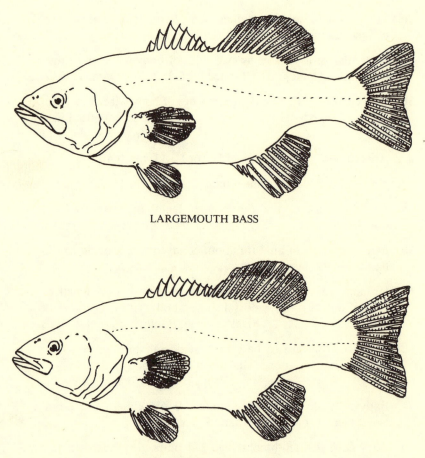

LARGEMOUTH BASS

SMALLMOUTH BASS

Figure 27. Lateral view of largemouth and smallmouth bass

9a. Mouth large, maxillary extends posterior to middle of eye; teeth on tongue .... Warmouth, *Lepomis gulosus*

9b. Mouth small, maxillary does not extend beyond middle of eye; no teeth on tongue 10

10a. Pectoral fin short and rounded and when laid forward only reaches eye (Figure 28) 11

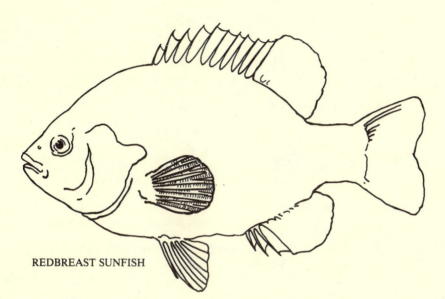

REDBREAST SUNFISH

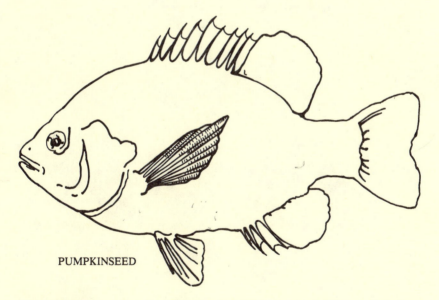

PUMPKINSEED

Figure 28. Pectoral fins of sunfish showing the short rounded form and the long pointed form

10b. Pectoral fin long and pointed and when laid forward almost reaches tip of snout (Figure 28) 13

11a. Opercular flap entirely black and not decorated with orange or red spots or bands.......................................12

11b. Opercular flap with red or orange spot or band at edge (appears white in preserved specimens).............. Longear sunfish, *Lepomis megalotis*

12a. Opercular flap as wide as long; gill rakers long (Figure 29) ..... Green sunfish, *Lepomis cyanellus*

12b. Opercular flap much longer than wide; gill rakers short (Figure 29)....................Redbreast sunfish, *Lepomis auritus*

13a. Opercular flap with bright red spot at posterior end, no dark spot at base of posterior dorsal fin; gill rakers short, thick, and sometimes curved (Figure 29) .... Pumpkinseed, *Lepomis gibbosus*

13b. Opercular flap entirely blue to margin, dark spot at base of posterior dorsal fin; gill rakers long and straight (Figure 29) ...... Bluegill, *Lepomis macrochirus*

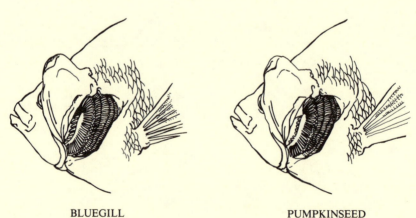

BLUEGILL   PUMPKINSEED

Figure 29. Gill rakers of bluegill and pumpkinseed sunfish

Rock Bass   *Ambloplites rupestris* (Rafinesque)

Identification

All sunfishes are distinguishable by the fact that they have 2 dorsal fins — an anterior spiny dorsal fin and a posterior soft dorsal — which are confluent, and that they have at least 3 spines in the anal fin. Several species have more than 3 anal spines. The rock bass, the black and white crappie, and the mud sunfish have 5–7 anal spines. The crappies are separated from the rock bass by the fact that the base of their anal and dorsal fins are of approximately the same length, whereas in rock bass the base of the anal fin is much shorter. The mud sunfish is distinguishable from the others by its rounded tail. Rock bass have a dark olive back and white undersides. Overlaying this background are irregular blotches and mottling above the lateral line and a series of 8–10 faint horizontal lines below the lateral line. The eye is red.

Life History

Rock bass spawn in early summer when the water has reached 60–70°F. The male constructs a plate-like depression in shallow water. The male guards the nest and waits for a female to join him. A female may carry 5,000 eggs or more, but generally she does not deposit them all in one nest. Instead she will visit several nests until she is spent. Accordingly, the male is likely to be visited by more than one female. The eggs hatch in 3–4 days, and not long after that they leave the nest and disperse. The male aggressively guards the nest during the time that his young are using it. Later in the summer, after the young have developed scales they are strikingly colored with large dark blotches.

Rock bass feed on insects, small fish, molluscs, and crayfish. They may live for more than 10 years, reaching one pound and a length of 13 inches. The usual size, however, is much smaller, about 8 or 9 inches and less than ½ pound. If overcrowded, they will be stunted, not even achieving this modest size.

Rock bass are found in rocky areas in lakes and in larger streams where they may be quite abundant. They are a frequent associate of the smallmouth bass and may compete with young bass for food.

Rock bass are easily caught by the angler. They will take flies, small spinners, or live bait. They fight well when first hooked, but quickly succumb. Their flesh is excellent, though bony.

Distribution

Rock bass are found from the Lake Champlain drainage west to the Dakotas and then south through the Mississippi Valley to the Gulf of Mexico. They are found in all the drainage systems in New York.

Other Names

Goggle-eye bass, redeye

Smallmouth Bass   *Micropterus dolomieui* Lacépède

Identification

Many people do not realize that the smallmouth and the largemouth black bass are members of the sunfish family and thus share the characteristics that distinguish this family from other freshwater fishes. Both the largemouth and smallmouth have 3 anal spines and a relatively elongate body whose standard length is 3–4½ times its greatest depth. The largemouth has a dark band running horizontally along its side which the smallmouth lacks. In addition, the notch between the first and second dorsal fin is deeper in the largemouth than the smallmouth and the posterior end of the upper jaw extends behind the orbit in the adult largemouth, but no further than the posterior edge of the orbit in the adult smallmouth. The back and sides are olive to grey shading into a light yellow-green on the lower flank. The undersides are greyish white.

Life History

Smallmouth spawn in May or early June over a gravel or rocky bottom. The male constructs a round nest where the female joins him and deposits several thousand eggs which the male fertilizes. She carries 5,000–7,000 eggs, and thus may visit other nests until she is spent. The male guards the nest, chasing any intruders away. The young hatch in 4–8 days and 2–3 weeks later they leave the nest as black fry.

Initially, smallmouth feed on microscopic crustaceans, switching to insects, crayfish, and fishes as they grow. Smallmouth may live for up to 14 or 15 years and reach 18–20 inches. The New York record smallmouth weighed 9 pounds and was taken in Friends Lake Outlet, Warren County, in 1925.

Smallmouth prefer cool water, with rock or gravel bottoms. They are found in both lakes and streams. In the spring they are in shallow water, but as the water warms they move into deeper water to escape the heat. During winter, under the ice, they remain rather listlessly near the bottom. They do not feed in winter and thus contribute nothing to the ice fishery.

The smallmouth is one of the species which makes angling in New York such a pleasure. It can be taken with wet or dry flies, spinners, spoons, plugs, or live bait such as crayfish, minnows, night crawlers, or hellgramites. When caught it puts up a magnificent fight with lots of leaping and aerial acrobatics. It is usually found in clear, cool streams or lakes and takes the bait actively.

Distribution

The original range of the smallmouth bass was the Great Lakes, St. Lawrence, and the Mississippi drainages. It has been widely introduced and is now found throughout the U.S., southern Canada, and in localities in Europe and Africa. It is found in all of the major drainages in New York.

Other Names

Smallmouth, black bass

Largemouth Bass   *Micropterus salmoides* (Lacépède)

Identification

The largemouth resembles the smallmouth in many ways. However, it has a fairly distinct, dark, wide band that extends horizontally along its side, except on very old individuals; a deep notch between the two dorsal fins; and a jaw which extends beyond the posterior margin of the eye, except in young individuals. The back and sides are olive to gray to black, grading to gray-white on the undersides. A dark band 5-7 scales rows wide extends down the side below the lateral line.

Life History

Largemouth bass spawn in late spring or early summer. They tend to choose shallower, weedier sites than the smallmouth, but other than this their spawning behavior is quite similar to the smallmouth. A female may carry up to 60,000 eggs, although the average is probably fewer than

10,000. The eggs hatch in 3–5 days, and it is another week before the fry are able to swim well enough to feed. They tend to remain together for another month with the male guarding them. At this early stage they are a light green color instead of the striking black color of smallmouth fry.

Largemouth begin life feeding on microscopic crustaceans, switch soon to insects, and eventually graduate to fish, frogs, worms, and crayfish. Individuals may live up to 15 years, some exceeding 20 inches and a weight of 8 pounds. The record for New York weighed 10 pounds, 12 ounces, and was taken from Chadwick Lake in 1975. More common, however, are 2–3 pound fish.

Largemouth bass are fish of quiet weedy water. They are common in shallow bays, small lakes, and ponds. They are rarely found in streams and rivers. They also seem to prefer siltier softer bottoms than the smallmouth. Consequently, even though the largemouth and smallmouth may both live in the same lake, they are seldom found in the same habitat. The largemouth will be in weedy bays, the smallmouth in deeper water with less vegetation.

The largemouth is an important game fish in New York. It is very common in small farm ponds as well as lakes. It can be taken on live bait or anything that resembles live bait; one of the more popular lures in recent years is the plastic night crawler. They can also be taken on spinners, plugs or spoons as well as flies or streamers.

Distribution

The original distribution of this species was the Great Lakes and Mississippi drainages and up the east coast from Florida to Virginia. Because of many introductions it is now found throughout the U.S. and also in the British Isles, France, Germany, South Africa, Brazil, the Philippines, and Hong Kong. In New York it is found in all major drainages.

Other Names

Bigmouth bass, largemouth

Black Crappie   *Pomoxis nigromaculatus* (LeSueur)

Identification

The crappies are the only other members of the sunfish family, besides the rock bass and mud sunfish, having 5–7 anal spines. They are easily distinguished by their shape and the fact that the base of their anal fin is about the same length as the base of their dorsal fin. Two species are known, the black crappie and the white crappie (*Pomoxis annularis*). The white crappie is quite rare in New York, but can be identified in that the distance from the base of the first dorsal spine to the eye is greater than the length of the base of the dorsal fin. In the black crappie these two distances are about equal. The back is green, olive, or gray, grading quickly to cream on the sides and belly. Overlaying this on the sides and median fins are a large number of irregular brown to black spots.

Life History

The black crappie spawns in early summer. Its habits are quite similar to other nest-building sunfish. Females may carry up to 150,000 eggs, but most have 20–50,000 eggs. Little is known about the early life history of this species. They apparently feed on plankton for the first few years, supplementing this with insect larvae. In later years they switch to fish, usually selecting individuals less than 2 inches long. Crappies may live for 8 or 9 years and reach a foot in length and a pound or more in weight. The record for New York is a 3-pound fish taken in Greenwood Lake.

Crappies are rarely if ever found in running water. They are lake or pond dwellers, prefering clear water with abundant vegetation. They tend to school and provide excellent fishing in the spring when they gather in pre-spawning congregations.

They can be taken on live bait, preferably small minnows, spinners or flies. One good method is to hook a minnow to a line, place a large bobber several feet up from the bait, and cast this toward a likely spot, allowing it to drift until a school is contacted. The action should be fast and furious after that. Although crappies are not large, they put up a respectable, albeit short, fight and they are delicious eating.

Distribution

The black crappie originally was found from Florida and Texas north to the Upper Mississippi Valley and Quebec. It too has been introduced beyond its normal range and is now commonly found throughout the U.S. In New York it is found in all of the major drainages.

Other Names

Crappie, calico bass, strawberry bass, Oswego bass

Redbreast Sunfish   *Lepomis auritus* (Linnaeus)

Identification

The fishes in the genus *Lepomis* are the ones that we most commonly think of as "sunfish." There are 3 species which are fairly common in the state: the redbreast, the pumpkinseed, and the bluegill. All three are distinguishable from other members of the sunfish family discussed earlier in that they have 3 anal spines and a deep body which is contained only 2–3 times in the standard length. The redbreast is distinguished from the bluegill and pumpkinseed by its short pectoral fin which, if laid forward, would reach no further than the eye. The bluegill and pumpkinseed have longer pectorals which, when laid forward, would almost reach the tip of the snout. The earflap on the redbreast is entirely blue. The pumpkinseed has a red spot on its earflap. Although the bluegill has a dark blue earflap like the redbreast, it has one distinguishing character that makes it easy to identify. At the posterior base of the dorsal fin is a dark spot. It looks as if someone had made a thumb print there. The back of the redbreast sunfish is olive to dark brown, the lower sides are gray to green, the belly gray-white, and the breast a bright orange. The opercular flap is dark blue. Turquoise bands radiate backward across the head.

Life History

The redbreast spawns in early summer constructing a nest in shallow water near shore or in a protected area in a stream. Females carry 1,000–8,000 eggs. The male guards the nest until the young hatch. Relatively little is known of the early life history of this species. It is a small fish reaching 6–8 inches under normal conditions. It feeds primarily on insects, but is known occasionally to consume small fish as well. During the winter they move into deeper water and form a wintering school which is relatively inactive all winter long.

The redbreast is too small to be a major sport fish. However, it does take bait or a lure readily and commonly appears in the catch of children fishing near shore.

Distribution

The range of this species extends from New Brunswick to Florida east of the Appalachians. In New York it is found in the Susquehanna, Delaware, Mohawk, and Hudson drainages, as well as Lake George.

Other Names

Red-bellied sunfish, bream, yellow belly sunfish, longear, bluegill

Pumpkinseed   *Lepomis gibbosus* (Linnaeus)

Identification

The pumpkinseed is readily distinguished from other sunfish in New York by the red spot on its earflap. It is extremely common and, along with the perch and bullhead, is probably the most familiar fish in the state. The back is olive to yellow-brown, shading to yellow or orange ventrally. The side of the head and cheek have several wavy turquoise bands.

Life History

Spawning occurs in early summer; the pattern is essentially the same as for other sunfish. A circular depression is created in shallow water by fanning with the tail and using the mouth to carry away larger objects. The nest usually has a diameter about twice the length of the fish constructing it. The male builds the nest and then the female comes to it. They swim together in a slow circle, emitting eggs and sperm which settle to the bottom of the nest. The male guards the nest and young until they disperse. A female may carry 1,500–3,000 eggs; and more than one female may spawn in a single nest. The males are very brightly colored at this time and defend the nest with great vigor. They are not easily frightened, and, in fact, a hand placed near the nest might get nipped.

Pumpkinseeds live for 8 or 9 years and rarely exceed 10 inches and ½ pound. They feed on insects, small invertebrates, molluscs, and occasionally a small fish. They are primarily residents of lakes and ponds, but also occur in quiet water in streams and rivers. They normally choose to live in or near vegetation or brush cover.

If for no other reason than the pumpkinseed has introduced thousands of young New Yorkers to the joy of angling, it would have to be considered an important species. However, the sunfish has proven to be a scrappy fighter when taken on light gear. It strikes flies, spinners, or live bait readily and puts up a good fight considering its size. The flesh is delicious, though bony.

Distribution

Originally, the pumpkinseed was found from New Brunswick to Georgia and west to the Dakotas. It has been widely introduced into many of the western states. In New York it is found in all of the major drainages.

Other Names

Pumpkinseed sunfish, common sunfish, sunfish, sunny

Bluegill   *Lepomis macrochirus* (Rafinesque)

Identification

The name bluegill is a good key to the identification of this species, but it is not sufficient since the redbreast sunfish has an entirely blue ear-flap also. The dusky thumbprint at the posterior edge of the soft dorsal is the other clue for positive identification. The back is dark green to brown, shading to white on the belly and yellow to orange on the breast.

Life History

Bluegills spawn in early summer as do the other sunfishes. Their behavior is very similar to the pumpkinseed and need not be repeated here. The young leave the nest when they are ¼ to ⅓ inch in length. There is evidence that at this very young age they leave the weedy shore of the lake and move into the open water zone of the lake where their transparent bodies provide good camouflage. At about an inch they have developed scales and now return to the vegetated portion of the lake. As young they feed on zooplankton, preferring cladocerans to copepods. Larger fish feed on insects, invertebrates, and, on occasion, small fish. They may live for 10 years, reaching 10 inches in length. Most individuals are between 6–9 inches long.

Bluegills tend to occupy more open habitat than the pumpkinseed even though both may be found in the same lake.

A great deal of enjoyment can be derived by using light gear when fishing for bluegill. Like the pumpkinseed they readily take flies, spinners, or bait and put up a solid fight when hooked. If you reduce your gear to match their capabilities, you will find that they will repay you with a strong fight. They are commonly stocked in farm ponds, but they have a tendency to become stunted if they are not fished very heavily.

Distribution

The bluegill was originally found in a region that extended from the St. Lawrence River south to Georgia and then west to Texas and Minnesota. It has been introduced in areas beyond this range. In New York it is found in the Allegheny, Great Lakes, Hudson, Delaware, Susquehanna, and Lake Champlain drainages, as well as on Long Island.

Other Names

Bluegill sunfish, bream

Selected Sunfish References

Breder, C. M., Jr. 1936. "I. The Reproductive Habits of the North American Sunfishes (Family Centrarchidae)." *Zoologica* 21(1): 1–48 + 1 pl.

Hile, R. 1941. "Age and Growth of the Rock Bass, *Ambloplites rupestris* (Rafinesque), in Nebish Lake, Wisconsin." *Trans. Wis. Acad. Sci. Arts Lett.* 33: 189–337.

Huish, M. T. 1954. "Life History of the Black Crappie of Lake George, Florida." *Trans. Amer. Fish Soc.* 83: 176–93.

Mraz, D., S. Kmiotek, and L. Frankenberger. 1961. "The Largemouth Bass. Its Life History, Ecology, and Management." *Wis. Conserv. Dep. Publ.* 232: 13 p.

Snow, H., A. Ensign, and J. Klingbiel. 1960. "The Bluegill. Its Life History, Ecology, and Management." *Wis. Conserv. Dep. Publ.* 230: 14 p.

Webster, D. W. 1954. "Smallmouth Bass, *Micropterus dolomieui*, in Cayuga Lake. (Part 1. Life History and Environment)." *Agr. Exp. Sta. Cornell Univ. Mem.* 327: 39 p.

Werner, R. G. 1969. "Ecology of Limnetic Bluegill Fry in Crane Lake, Indiana." *Amer. Midl. Nat.* 81: 164–81.

————. 1972. "Bluespotted Sunfish, *Enneacanthus gloriosus*, in Lake Ontario Drainage." *Copeia* 1972(4): 878–79.

Perch   Family Percidae

Members of the perch family are small to moderately large physoclistus fishes with ctenoid scales, two separate dorsal fins, and one or two spines in the anal fin.

The family is composed of 126 species, of which 16 are found in New York. We will discuss only 5 of the most common species.

Species Key

1a. Preoperculum with serrated edge (Figure 30); mouth large, maxillary extends to at least middle of eye; adults usually longer than 6 inches 2

1b. Preoperculum smooth; mouth small, maxillary extends only to anterior edge of eye; adults usually less than 5 inches 4

2a. No canine teeth present on lower jaw, i.e., all teeth are of about the same length, none protruding; anal soft rays 6–8; dorsal soft rays 12–13 . . . . Yellow perch, *Perca flavescens*

2b. Canine teeth present on lower jaw (Figure 31), anal soft rays 11–14, dorsal soft rays 17–23 3

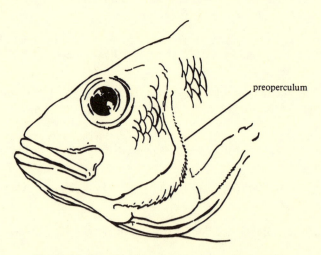

Figure 30. Serrated preoperculum on yellow perch

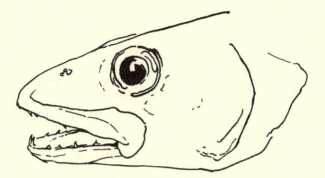

Figure 31. Canine teeth on walleye.

3a. Distinct round black spots on spinous dorsal; no black blotch at
posterior base of spinous dorsal fin; dorsal soft rays 17–21 . . . .
Sauger, *Stizostedion canadense*

3b. Diffuse black markings on spinous dorsal; large black blotch at
posterior base of spinous dorsal fin; dorsal soft rays 19–23 . . . .
Walleye, *Stizostedion vitreum*

4a. Body translucent and partially naked, scales found on midline
of sides, rest of body without scales; slender, body depth is contained 7 or more times in standard length . . Eastern sand darter,
Ammocrypta pellucida

4b. Body opaque and completely scaled; more robust, body depth
is contained less than 7 times in standard length 5

5a. Midline of body contains a distinct row of specialized scales
separated from scales on either side by small groove; space between pelvic fins is at least 3/4 as wide as base of pelvic fins;
area of anal fin about equal to area of second dorsal 6

5b. Midline of belly without specialized scale row; space between
pelvic fins less than 3/4 pelvic base; area of anal fin less than
area of second dorsal 11

6a. Premaxilla protractile (Figure 16) . . . . Channel darter,
Percina copelandi

6b. Premaxilla not protractile (Figure 16) 7

7a. Snout conical and extending beyond upper lip; sides of body with 14–16 vertical bars, every other one expanded at lower end .... Logperch, *Percina caprodes*

7b. Snout not extending beyond upper lip; sides of body with dark blotches that tend to run together along lateral line 8

8a. Cheeks completely scaleless 9

8b. Cheeks more or less scaled .... Blackside darter, *Percina maculata*

9a. More than 70 scales in lateral line .... Longhead darter, *Percina macrocephala*

9b. Fewer than 65 scales in lateral line 10

10a. Color olive and bronze; 7 dark blotches more or less confluent along lateral line .... Gilt darter, *Percina evides*

10b. Color pale yellow; 6 dark blotches usually not confluent along lateral line .... Shield darter, *Percina peltata*

11a. Premaxillaries protractile 12

11b. Premaxillaries not protractile 14

12a. Two anal spines .... Greenside darter, *Etheostoma blennioides*

12b. One anal spine (first soft ray is unbranched and thus resembles a spine, but it is segmented) 13

13a. Six or seven *X* or *W* markings on side; 10–12 rays in second dorsal fin .... Johnny darter, *Etheostoma nigrum*

13b. Nine to eleven *X* or *W* markings on side; 12–14 rays in second dorsal fin .... Tesselated darter, *Etheostoma olmstedi*

14a. Lateral line incomplete, normally not extending beyond posterior end of soft dorsal fin 15

14b. Lateral line complete or nearly so, lacking only last 5 or 6 scales 18

15a. No more than 3 scale rows between lateral line and base of spinous dorsal .... Swamp darter, *Etheostoma fusiforme*

15b. At least 4 scale rows between lateral line and base of spinous dorsal 16

16a. Shoulder region containing a markedly enlarged black humeral scale; spinous dorsal low, about ½ height of soft dorsal, knobs on tips of spines in males .... Fantail darter,
Etheostoma flabellare

16b. Shoulder region without a black humeral scale; spinous dorsal nearly as high as soft dorsal 17

17a. Cheeks almost naked, opercles with scales .... Rainbow darter,
Etheostoma caeruleum

17b. Both cheeks and opercles more or less scaled ..... Iowa darter,
Etheostoma exile

18a. Gill covers not at all united by a membrane extending across the isthmus 19

18b. Gill covers broadly connected by a membrane extending across the isthmus 20

19a. Relatively small scales, more than 55 scale rows in body length .... Spotted darter, *Etheostoma maculatum*

19b. Relatively large scales, fewer than 55 scale rows in body length .... Rainbow darter, *Etheostoma caeruleum*

20a. 12 or more dorsal spines.................... Variegate darter,
Etheostoma variatum

20b. Fewer than 12 dorsal spines .... Banded darter,
Etheostoma zonale

Yellow Perch   *Perca flavescens* (Mitchill)

Identification

Perch are quickly recognized by the yellow background color on their sides which is interrupted by broad vertical olive green bands. Even more dependable is the fact that they have two separate dorsal fins; an anterior spiny dorsal fin and a posterior soft dorsal fin. The anal fin has only 2 spines and 6-8 soft rays. The preoperculum has a serrated edge and the teeth are all uniform in size, i.e., there are no canine teeth.

Life History

Spawning occurs in early spring when the water has warmed up to at least 44°F and before it reaches 54°F. Adults move into shallow water sometimes entering tributary streams. Spawning occurs at night over brush or vegetation. A single female leads a long double line of males around a circuitous course and eventually extrudes a long gelatinous string of eggs which is fertilized by the attendant males. No nest is built, but the eggs are retained and protected in a unique and very interesting way. The eggs are contained in a long (up to 7 feet) gelatinous tube. The tube is folded like a partially extended accordion. The egg mass is semi-buoyant and tends to move with the oscillation of the water. Such movement creates a pumping action which draws water into the hollow center of the tube and expels stale water through small inconspicuous holes along its length. This system is clearly an adaptation for providing the eggs protection from mechanical shock and desiccation, but it also aerates them. It is somewhat reminiscent of the bullhead egg mass, except that the bullhead had to work very hard to keep enough water flowing over the eggs to insure proper aeration. Each female may carry from 3,000 to 100,000 eggs depending on her size, the average being approximately 20–30,000. The young hatch in a week to 10 days and remain close to the bottom and relatively inactive until the yolk sac is absorbed. They begin feeding on zooplankton, switching to small insects before the end of their first year. As adults, they continue to eat insects, but they also feed on crayfish and small fish as well. Perch live for about 8 or 9 years and grow to 10 to 11 inches; they become sexually mature at 3 or 4 years.

Perch are shallow water fish and move in large, loosely organized groups. They are inactive at night and can be seen on a summer evening resting on the bottom by simply shining a powerful light into the water. They do not become inactive in the winter, but continue to move and feed under the ice.

Of all the different kinds of fish in New York, the yellow perch would have to rate very near the top in numbers caught by fishermen. It is not a good fighting fish, but it is easily caught and very good eating. It is most often taken on live bait, fished just off the bottom and it can be taken winter or summer.

Perch have a tendency to become stunted if their populations get too large for the food supply. They also compete successfully with salmonids for food, and thus create difficulties in the management of trout fisheries.

In addition to providing food and sport for man, perch are an important forage fish for many large game fish. The walleye fishery in Oneida Lake, for example, is largely dependent on young perch as a food base.

Distribution

The yellow perch ranges from Nova Scotia to Florida, then westward in a broad band to Montana and Great Slave Lake. In New York it is found in all major drainages.

Other Names

Perch, jackperch

Walleye   *Stizostedion vitreum* (Mitchill)

Identification

Walleyes are large perch-like fish with serrations on the posterior edge of their preoperculum, a forked tail, and canine teeth in the lower jaw. Adults do not have the regular dark vertical bars like the perch but, instead, have a pattern of irregular dark blotches on a brown to yellow background. The first dorsal fin of the walleye has a characteristic large black spot at its posterior base, and the tip of the lower lobe of the caudal fin is whitish. This distinguishes walleyes from saugers which are missing the large spot on the dorsal fin and the white spot on the caudal fin, but have many smaller black spots scattered over the entire first dorsal, usually arranged in horizontal rows.

Stizostedion vitreum is composed of two subspecies, the walleye and the blue pike. The blue pike was formerly found in New York waters, but is now so rare that it is listed as an endangered species. In fact, some ichthyologists believe that it is actually extinct.

Life History

Walleyes spawn in the spring just after the ice leaves the lake and tributary streams. They choose sites in streams with good flow and gravel bottoms or remain in lakes spawning over gravel shoals. Males normally arrive first, followed later by the larger females. Eggs are broadcast over the bottom; no nests are built. The eggs sink to the bottom, becoming entangled in vegetation or falling into spaces between the rocks. A large female may lay more than half a million eggs. Survival to hatching is not good, however, if 20 percent of the eggs hatch this is an excellent survival rate. More commonly less than 5 percent of the eggs hatch under natural conditions. This would still leave 25,000 fry from a female which produced 500,000 eggs. In a stable population you would expect 24,998 of these fry to die before they reach sexual maturity. Because of this high mortality rate of the eggs it has become a common management practice to take eggs from walleyes, fertilize them, and incubate them in a hatchery until they hatch. They are usually stocked shortly thereafter. When this is done survival is greatly increased. Under natural conditions the eggs hatch in 2–2½ weeks and the young fish encumbered by their yolk sac drift into deeper water.

They feed initially on zooplankton but switch to small fish in a short while. In Oneida Lake, where walleye have been studied for many years, it is clear that they depend heavily on young perch for food. Perch spawn a few weeks after the walleye, and perch fry appear in the lake just about the time young walleye are switching from zooplankton to fish. They continue this beneficial relationship (from the walleye's point of view) throughout their lives. Walleyes will feed on other forage fish as well and even, on occasion, insects. Walleye feed primarily during periods of darkness or low light. The inside of their eye is lined with a reflective surface called the tapetum lucidum which allows them to see quite well in the dark. It is the tapetum lucidum which causes the eye shine observed when a walleye is brought into a lighted boat at night.

Walleye may live up to 15 years and achieve a weight of 25 pounds. The largest fish taken by an angler in New York was 15 pounds, 3 ounces, and it was taken from the Chemung River in 1952. More commonly the walleye caught by fishermen is less than 3 pounds and only 3 or 4 years old.

Large lakes and rivers are the preferred habitat of walleyes. It is rarely found in lakes less than 100 acres in size. In addition, if the lake is a bit turbid, thus reducing the light that penetrates the water, the walleye seems to do better. The tapetum lucidum, which is very useful when light intensities are low, causes the fish to be very sensitive to high-intensity light. Thus clear lakes with good light penetration are poor habitats for walleyes.

Walleyes generally move in groups, usually near the bottom. They are active throughout the year and thus are an important species to the ice fisherman.

To the angler and the commercial fisherman the walleye is one of the most highly prized fish. Its flesh is light and tasty. Although not a spectacular fighting fish, it achieves a large enough size that catching a walleye is always a thrill.

Distribution

It ranges from Quebec south, west of the Appalachians, to the Gulf

Coast, and then northwestward to the MacKenzie River. In New York it is found in all of the major drainages save Long Island.

Other Names

Walleyed pike, yellow pike, pike perch

Sauger   *Stizostedion canadense* (Smith)

Identification

The sauger resembles a walleye except that it does not have the dusky spot on the posterior base of its first dorsal fin, or the white spot on the lower lobe of its caudal fin. It does have several rows of fairly distinct black spots on the membranes of the first dorsal fin. These spots, however, are considerably smaller than the large dark blotch in the walleye. The body is basically a light brown overlaid with darker brown blotches.

Life History

Sauger spawn in the spring, just slightly later than the walleye and in roughly the same type of habitat. While sauger prefer even larger bodies of water, their life history is quite similar to the walleye.

Distribution

Sauger are found in a region that extends from the St. Lawrence River to Alabama and north to Alberta. Sauger are not abundant in New York. They are moderately common in Lake Erie and Lake Champlain. They may also be rarely encountered in other large bodies of water such as the St. Lawrence River, Lake Ontario, and the larger Finger Lakes.

Other Name

Sand pike

Tesselated Darter   *Etheostoma olmstedi* Storer

Identification

The tesselated darter, a member of the perch family, has two separate dorsal fins. The anterior is composed entirely of spines, the posterior entirely of soft rays. There is a single spine in the anal fin. The spines in the darters are quite soft and flexible and easily confused with rays unless one look carefully for the lack of segmentation or the lack of flaring at the end. All darters are distinguishable from perch, walleye, and sauger by the smooth edge on their preoperculum, the rounded tail and small size. There are 17 species of darters known in New York in 3 genera. They are somewhat difficult to identify. The tesselated darter is common and easily recognized, however, by the presence of a series of 9 to 11 X, W, M, or V-shaped dark marks running horizontally along its side. The background color is a light brown or straw color occasionally with a green tinge.

Life History

Spawning takes place in late April or May in shallow streams with rocky bottoms. Males enter the spawning area first and establish territories which they defend vigorously. When the females are ready to spawn they enter the spawning area and are met by a territorial male. Eggs are laid by the female on the underside of a rock. She moves upside down along the rock accompanied by the male. As she extrudes eggs they are fertilized. Normally 30–200 eggs are laid by each female. After spawning the male stands guard over the nest and fans it to keep water circulating over the eggs. The eggs hatch in 5–8 days.

Darters feed on microscopic crustaceans and small insects as well as organic debris from the bottom. They live for 3 or 4 years and reach about 2½ inches when full grown.

They are widespread throughout the state, generally preferring running water with a sandy bottom. They may also be found near shore or stream mouths in lakes and ponds, and over silty or gravelly bottoms.

None of the darters are of significance to sport or commercial fishermen by themselves, but they may serve as forage to a number of game species. They are an interesting fish to observe in an aquarium and are relatively hardy.

Distribution

The tesselated darter is found east of the Appalachians from the St. Lawrence River to North Carolina. In New York it is found in the Hudson, Delaware, Susquehanna, Long Island, and Great Lakes drainages.

Other Name

Johnny darter

Logperch   *Percina caprodes* (Rafinesque)

Identification

The logperch is a darter and has all of the distinctive darter characteristics—small size, smooth preoperculum, and rounded or at least non-forked tail. The logperch is distinguishable from all of the darters in the genus *Etheostoma* by the fact that when viewed from the side its anal fin is as large as its posterior dorsal fin. In *Etheostoma* the anal fin is smaller. The logperch is readily distinguished from the eastern sand darter, *Ammocrypta*, since the sand darter's body is rather clear and transparent, unlike the normally colored logperch. In addition, the sand darter has only one anal spine, whereas the logperch has two anal spines. The logperch is separated from the other members of the genus *Percina* by its long snout which protrudes beyond its upper lip and by the fact that the markings on its side are dark vertical bars instead of large blotches. The background color is yellow-green.

Life History

Logperch are primarily a lake-dwelling species, but they are also known from large streams and rivers. They spawn late in June, moving in from deep water to water less than 6 feet deep. Males congregate in a large group of several hundred individuals over a sandy bottom. Periodically, a female will enter this group and swim circuitously through it. She will be followed by many males, one of which will catch up with her. Then they settle to the bottom, the male resting on the back of the female. They both make violent movements with their bodies, creating a small pit in the sand and throwing up a large sand cloud in the process; 10–20 eggs are laid and fertilized at this time, and they fall back into the pit and are covered by the settling sand. Any eggs that are not covered are eaten by waiting males. This process continues until the female has spawned many times. She carries from 1,000 to 3,000 eggs but whether she deposits all of them during spawning is unknown. No parental care of the eggs after spawning has been observed.

The young feed on microscopic crustaceans, switching to insects as they grow. Adults feed primarily on insects and are reported to use their long snout to poke under leaves and turn rocks over in a search for food. Adults may reach 4–5 inches when fully grown.

Distribution

The logperch can be found from the St. Lawrence River south on the western side of the Appalachians to the Gulf of Mexico and northwest to Saskatchewan. In New York it is found in all major drainages except the Delaware, Susquehanna, and Long Island systems.

Other Names

Zebra fish, manitou darter

Selected Perch References

Forney, J. L. 1967. "Estimates of Biomass and Mortality Rates in a Walleye Population." *N.Y. Fish Game J.* 14: 176–92.

Raney, E. C., and E. A. Lachner. 1942. "Studies of the Summer Food, Growth, and Movements of Young Yellow Pike-Perch, *Stizostedion v. vitreum*, in Oneida Lake, New York. *J. Wildlife Manage.* 6: 1–16.

_____. 1943. "Age and Growth of Johnny Darters, *Boleosoma nigrum olmstedi* (Storer) and *Boleosoma longimanum* (Jordan)." *Amer. Midland Natur.* 29: 229–38.

Winn, H. E. 1958. "Comparative Reproductive Behavior and Ecology of Fourteen Species of Darters (Pisces — Percidae)." *Ecol. Monogr.* 28: 155–91.

Drum   Family Sciaenidae

The drums are stout physoclistus fishes with ctenoid scales, and a lateral line that extends onto the caudal fin. About 160 species belong to this primarily marine family, of which one is known from New York.

Freshwater Drum   *Aplodinotus grunniens* (Rafinesque)

Identification

The freshwater drum is the only member of the family Sciaenidae found in inland waters in New York. Other species in the family are marine. The drum bears a resemblance to the carp in that it is a heavy-bodied fish; however, the drum has 8–9 spines in the anterior dorsal fin; 2 spines in the anal fin, one small, the second quite large; and a lateral line that extends well onto a rounded caudal fin. Basically, the drum is a silvery fish with a green to brown back and white undersides.

Life History

The spawning and early life history of the drum is not well known. Some investigators believe that the drum spawns in shallow water in the spring or early summer, producing demersal eggs that stick to the bottom. Other scientists have evidence suggesting that the eggs float and are pelagic. In either case, the eggs hatch in a day or two and the young begin feeding on minute crustaceans. As they get older and larger they switch to feeding on molluscs, for which they are well adapted. They have large powerful sets of teeth in their pharynx which they use to crush the shell of the snail or clam, and then they spit out the shell and swallow the soft body. They also feed on insects, crayfish, and small fish.

Drum commonly range in size from 1 to 5 pounds. However, specimens are known which exceeded 35 pounds. Maximum age for the species is 15-20 years.

Deep water is the habitat for drum, particularly where the water is clean and the bottom well supplied with food. They normally remain near the bottom and are known to move shoreward at dusk. Drum are never found in small streams or small lakes. They inhabit large lakes and deep pools in large rivers.

The freshwater drum has a tendency to make a grunting noise which is quite audible to the human ear. This noise is made not with vocal cords as in humans, but by vibrating the swim bladder, creating sound waves that pass through the water. The function of this sound is unknown, but since it occurs most noticeably during the spawning season, it is felt that it may play some role in courtship behavior.

The ear stones (otoliths) of the drum are interesting also. They are large and marked with an L-shaped groove that resembles a boomerang. Many people people have discovered these on a beach and considered them lucky charms.

Very few anglers fish for drum, but those who do appreciate the fact that it is a strong, if not spectacular fighter. It can be taken on artificial lures or live bait fished near the bottom. The flesh is of average quality and flavor.

Distribution

The drum is found in the Great Lakes drainage and the Mississippi

Valley. In New York it is found in Lakes Erie, Ontario, Champlain, and Oneida.

Other Names

Sheepshead, croaker, grunt, drum

Selected Drum Reference

Edsal, T. A. 1967. "Biology of the Freshwater Drum in Western Lake Erie." *Ohio J. Sci.* 67(6): 321–40.

General References

Carlander, K. D. 1969. *Handbook of Freshwater Fishery Biology*, vol. 1. Ames: Iowa State University Press, 752 p.

_____. 1977. *Handbook of Freshwater Fishery Biology*, vol. 2. Ames: Iowa State University Press, 431 p.

Eddy, S. 1969. *How to Know the Freshwater Fishes*. Dubuque, Iowa: William C. Brown, 286 p.

_____, and T. Surber. 1960. *Northern Fishes with Special Reference to the Upper Mississippi Valley*. Mass.: Charles T. Branford, 276 p.

Everhart, W. H. 1958. *Fishes of Maine*. Maine Dept. Inland Fish and Game.

Forbes, S. A., and R. E. Richardson. 1920. *The Fishes of Illinois*. Illinois Natural History Survey. 357 p.

Gerking, S. D. 1945. "The Distribution of the Fishes of Indiana." *Invest. Ind. Lakes and Streams* 3(1): 1–37.

_____. 1967. *The Biological Basis of Freshwater Fish Production*. Oxford: Blackwell. 495 p.

Greeley, J. R. 1927. "Fishes of the Region with Annotated List." *A Biological Survey of the Genesee River System*. Suppl 16th Ann. Rep. N.Y. Conserv. Dept., 47–66.

_____. 1928. "Fishes of the Oswego Watershed with Annotated List." *A Biological Survey of the Oswego River System*. Suppl. 17th Ann. Rep. N.Y. Conserv. Dept., 84–107.

_____. 1929. "Fishes of the Erie-Niagara Watershed with Annotated List." *A Biological Survey of the Erie-Niagara System*." Suppl. 18th Ann. Rep. N.Y. Conserv. Dept., 150–79.

178

_____. 1930. "Fishes of the Lake Champlain Watershed." *A Biological Survey of the Champlain Watershed.* Suppl. 19th Ann. Rep. N.Y. Conserv. Dept., 44–87.

_____. 1934. "Fishes of the Raquette Watershed with Annotated List."*A Biological Survey of the Raquette Watershed.* Suppl. 23rd Ann. Rep. N.Y. Conserv. Dept., 53–108.

_____. 1935. "Fishes of the Watershed with Annotated List." *A Biological Survey at the Mohawk-Hudson Watershed.* Suppl. 24th Ann. Rep. N.Y. Conserv. Dept., 63–101.

_____. 1936. "Fishes of the Area with Annotated List." *A Biological Survey of the Delaware and Susquehanna Watersheds.* Suppl. 25th Ann. Rep. N.Y. Conserv. Dept., 45–88.

_____. 1937. "Fishes of the Area with Annotated List." *A Biological Survey of the Lower Hudson Watershed.* Suppl. 26th Ann. Rep. N.Y. Conserv. Dept., 45–103.

_____. 1938. "Fishes of the Area with Annotated List." *A Biological Survey of the Allegheny and Chemung Watersheds.* Suppl. 27th Ann. Rep. N.Y. Conserv. Dept., 48–73.

_____. 1939. "The Freshwater Fishes of Long Island." Suppl. 28th Ann. Rep. N.Y. Conserv. Dept.

_____. 1940. "Fishes of the Watershed with Annotated List." *A Biological Survey of the Lake Ontario Watershed.* Suppl. 29th Ann. Rep. N.Y. Conserv. Dept., 42–81.

Greeley, J. R., and S. C. Bishop. 1932. "Fishes of the Area with Annotated List." *A Biological Survey of the Oswegatchie and Black River Systems.* Suppl. 21st Ann. Rep. N.Y. Conserv. Dept., 54–93.

_____. 1933. "Fishes of the Upper Hudson Watershed with Annotated List." *A Biological Survey of the Upper Hudson Watershed.* Suppl. 22nd Ann. Rep. N.Y. Conserv. Dept., 64–101.

Greeley, J. R., and C. W. Greene. 1931. "Fishes of the Area with Annotated List." *A Biological Survey of the St. Lawrence Watershed.* Suppl. 20th Ann. Rep. N.Y. Conserv. Dept., 44–94.

Greenwood, P. H., D. E. Rosen, S. H. Weitzman, and G. S. Myers. 1966. "Phyletic Studies of Teleostean Fishes, with a Provisional Classification of Living Forms." *Bull. Amer. Mus. Natur. Hist.* 131(4):339–456.

Harlan, J. R., and E. B. Speaker. 1969. *Iowa Fish and Fishing.* State Conserv. Comm. Des Moines, Iowa. 365 p.

Hubbs, C. L., and G. P. Cooper. 1936. "Minnows of Michigan." *Cranbrook Inst. Sci. Bull.* 8. 95 p.

Hubbs, C. L., and K. F. Lagler. 1964. *Fishes of the Great Lakes Region.* Ann Arbor: University of Michigan Press, 213 pp.

Kendall, W. C., and W. A. Dence. 1929. "The Fishes of the Cranberry Lake Region." *Roosevelt Wildlife Bull.* 5(2):219–309.

Lagler, K. F., J. E. Bardach, and R. R. Miller. 1962. *Ichthyology.* New York: Wiley. 545 p.

Legendre, V. 1954. *Key to Game and Commercial Fishes of the Province of Quebec.* Vol. 1, *The Freshwater Fishes.* Montreal: Soc. Can. d'Ecole. 180 p.

Livingstone, D. A. 1953. "The Freshwater Fishes of Nova Scotia." *Proc. Nova Scotian Inst. Sci.* 23(1):90 p.

MacKay, H. H. 1963. *Fishes of Ontario.* Toronto: Ont. Dept. Lands and Forests. 300 p.

Marshall, N. B. 1966. *The Life of Fishes.* Cleveland: World. 402 p.

————. 1971. *Explorations in the Life of Fishes.* Cambridge: Harvard University Press. 204 p.

McClane, A. J., ed. 1965. *McClane's Standard Fishing Encyclopedia and International Angling Guide.* New York: Holt, Rinehart and Winston. 105 p.

Moore, G. A. 1968. "Fishes." *Vertebrates of the United States,* W. F. Blair, et al. 2nd ed. New York: McGraw-Hill, pp. 21–165.

Nelson, J. S. 1976. *Fishes of the World.* New York: Wiley. 416 p.

Nikolsky, G. V. 1954; rev. 1961. *Special Ichthyology.* Washington, D.C.: Nat. Sci. Found. and Smithsonian Institution. 538 p.

————. 1963. *The Ecology of Fishes.* New York: Academic. 352 p.

Norman, J. R. 1963. *A History of Fishes,* 2nd ed. Rev. by P. H. Greenwood. London: Ernest Benn. 398 p.

Scott, W. G. 1967. *Freshwater Fishes of Eastern Canada,* 2nd ed. Toronto: University of Toronto Press. 137 p.

Scott, W. B., and E. J. Crossman. 1973. *Freshwater Fishes of Canada. Fisheries Research Bd. Can. Bull.* 184: 966 p.

Trautman, M. 1957. *The Fishes of Ohio with Illustrated Keys.* Ohio: Ohio State University Press, 683 p.

Whitworth, W. R., P. L. Berrien, and W. T. Keller. 1968. "Freshwater Fishes of Connecticut." *State Geol. and Nat. Hist. Surv. of Conn. Bull.* 101. 134 p.

Index

186

SUNY College of Environmental Science
   and Forestry, 117
Susquehanna River, 49, 62

Umbra limi, 6, 96
   pygmaea, 6, 95
Upper Saranac Lake, 77

Togue. *See* Trout, lake
Tomcod, 12, 135
Topminnow. *See* Killifish, banded
Trout, brook, 3, 6, 65, 69–70, 73
   brown, 6, 65, 68, 70, 77, Fig. 12
   lake, 6, 65, 69, 76
   rainbow, 6, 65, 68–69, 80
Troutperch, 12, 134
Tupper Lake, 73
Twin Lake, 85
Tyee. *See* Salmon, chinook

Walleye, 16, 165, 169, Fig. 31
Walton, Izaak, 78
Warmouth, 14, 152
West Canada Lake, 77
Whitefish, lake, 5, 65–66, 71, Figs. 10-11
   round, 5, 65–66, 70, Fig. 10
Windfish. *See* Fallfish
Wolf Lake, 77

Zebra fish. *See* Logperch